Collaborating for Climate Equity

This book explores the capacity of different stakeholders to work together and build urban resilience to climate change through an equity-centered approach to cross-sectoral collaboration.

Urban areas, where the majority of the global population dwells, are particularly vulnerable to a myriad of climate stressors, the effects of which are acutely present in places and to communities that have been largely excluded from decision-making processes. Our need for working and learning together is at a critical threshold, yet at present, the process for and understanding of inter-sectoral collaborations remains a theoretical ideal and falls short of the broad appeal that many have claimed. *Collaborating for Climate Equity* argues that researcher–practitioner partnerships offer a promising pathway toward ensuring equitable outcomes while building climate resilience. By presenting five case studies from the United States, Chile, and Mexico, each chapter explores the contours of developing robust researcher–practitioner collaborations that endure and span institutional boundaries. The case studies included in the book are augmented by a synthesis that reflects upon the key findings and offers generalizable principles for applying similar approaches to other cities across the globe.

This work contributes to a nascent knowledge base on the real-world challenges and opportunities associated with researcher–practitioner partnerships. It provides guidance to academics and practitioners involved in collaborative research, planning, and policymaking.

Vivek Shandas is a professor of climate transformation and founding director of the Sustaining Urban Places Research (SUPR) Lab at Portland State University. Professor Shandas studies the effects of urban development patterns and processes on ecosystems and social justice. He has published over 100 articles and three books, and his research has been featured in the *New York Times*, National Geographic, *Scientific American*, and dozens of other international and local media. During his spare time he revels in the mountains and waters of the Pacific Northwest with his family.

Dana Hellman is an environmental social scientist and holds a PhD degree in Earth, Environment & Society. Her work addresses topics spanning climate change risk and adaptation, environmental health, resource management, and nature conservation, as well as intersections among them. She delights in making unexpected connections and synthesizing information across fields and takes an interdisciplinary approach to research and analysis, drawing upon complementary theories and practices from social and environmental sciences. Her work emphasizes themes including resilience, power/knowledge dynamics, collaborative approaches, and (sense of) place. Dana is passionate about translating theory into practice, applying research to real-world problems, and pursuing social justice through environmental action.

Routledge Focus on Environment and Sustainability

German Radioactive Waste
Changes in Policy and Law
Robert Rybski

The Sustainable Manifesto
A Commitment to Individual, Economical, and Political Change
Kersten Reich

Phyto and Microbial Remediation of Heavy Metals and Radionuclides in the Environment
An Eco-Friendly Solution for Detoxifying Soils
Rym Salah-Tazdaït and Djaber Tazdaït

Water Governance in Bolivia
Cochabamba since the Water War
Nasya Sara Razavi

Indigenous Identity, Human Rights and the Environment in Myanmar
Local Engagement with Global Rights Discourses
Jonathan Liljeblad

Participatory Design and Social Transformation
Images and Narratives of Crisis and Change
John A. Bruce

Collaborating for Climate Equity
Researcher–Practitioner Partnerships in the Americas
Edited by Vivek Shandas and Dana Hellman

For more information about this series, please visit: www.routledge.com/Routledge-Focus-on-Environment-and-Sustainability/book-series/RFES

Collaborating for Climate Equity
Researcher–Practitioner Partnerships in the Americas

Edited by Vivek Shandas and Dana Hellman

First published 2022
by Routledge
4 Park Square, Milton Park, Abingdon, Oxon OX14 4RN

and by Routledge
605 Third Avenue, New York, NY 10158

Routledge is an imprint of the Taylor & Francis Group, an informa business

© 2022 selection and editorial matter, Vivek Shandas and Dana Hellman; individual chapters, the contributors

The right of Vivek Shandas and Dana Hellman to be identified as the authors of the editorial material, and of the authors for their individual chapters, has been asserted in accordance with sections 77 and 78 of the Copyright, Designs and Patents Act 1988.

All rights reserved. No part of this book may be reprinted or reproduced or utilised in any form or by any electronic, mechanical, or other means, now known or hereafter invented, including photocopying and recording, or in any information storage or retrieval system, without permission in writing from the publishers.

Trademark notice: Product or corporate names may be trademarks or registered trademarks, and are used only for identification and explanation without intent to infringe.

British Library Cataloguing-in-Publication Data
A catalogue record for this book is available from the British Library

Library of Congress Cataloging-in-Publication Data
A catalog record has been requested for this book

ISBN: 978-1-032-07774-1 (hbk)
ISBN: 978-1-032-10137-8 (pbk)
ISBN: 978-1-003-20872-3 (ebk)

DOI: 10.4324/9781003208723

Typeset in Times New Roman
by Apex CoVantage, LLC

Contents

List of Contributors vii

1 An introduction to researcher–practitioner partnerships for climate equity 1
DANA HELLMAN & VIVEK SHANDAS

2 Designing urban greenspace from the grassroots up: The *'barrio* innovation' approach 17
MARTA BERBÉS-BLÁZQUEZ, VANYA BISHT,
REGIONAL CARRILLO, MONIQUE FRANCO,
MANDY KUHN & JORGE MORALES-GUERRERO

3 Envisioning future scenarios to manage pluvial flooding in social-ecological-technological systems 36
JASON SAUER, OLGA BARBOSA, ELIZABETH M. COOK,
NANCY GRIMM, CRISTÓBAL LAMARCA, JAVIERA MAIRA,
ALEJANDRA SCHUEFTAN & DAVID M. IWANIEC

4 Co-evolution of resilience initiatives toward a resilience collaboration 54
TIFFANY G. TROXLER & JANE GILBERT

5 Operational guidelines for the identification of green infrastructure in a semiarid city 67
AGUSTIN ROBLES-MORÚA, EDUARDO HINOJOSA-ROBLES,
JAVIER NAVARRO-ESTUPIÑÁN, DIANA MEZA FIGUEROA,
EFRAIN VIZUETE JARAMILLO & MARÍA G. PEÑÚÑURI

6 **Community science for the (climate) win: An equity-based framework for understanding and acting on extreme urban heat** 85
JEREMY S. HOFFMAN, VIVEK SHANDAS & LARA JOHNSON

7 **Conclusion: Common themes, lessons learned, and next steps** 101
VIVEK SHANDAS & DANA HELLMAN

Contributors

Olga Barbosa is an affiliate of Austral University of Chile (Universidad Austral de Chile) and the Ministry of Science, Technology, Knowledge and Innovation of Chile (Ministerio de Ciencia, Tecnología, Conocimiento, e Innovación de Chile).

Marta Berbés-Blázquez is an affiliate of School for the Future of Innovation in Society, Arizona State University, USA; Central Arizona Phoenix Long Term Ecological Research (CAP LTER), USA; and School of Planning and Faculty of Environment, University of Waterloo, Canada.

Vanya Bisht is an affiliate of School for the Future of Innovation in Society, Arizona State University, USA, and Central Arizona Phoenix Long Term Ecological Research (CAP LTER), USA.

Regional Carrillo is an affiliate of Academia del Pueblo, USA.

Elizabeth M. Cook is an affiliate of Barnard College, USA.

Diana Meza Figueroa is an affiliate of Universidad de Sonora, Dirección de Vinculación y Difusión, Departamento de Geología, México.

Monique Franco is an affiliate of Central Arizona Phoenix Long Term Ecological Research (CAP LTER), USA.

Jane Gilbert is an affiliate of Miami Dade County, USA; Miami Dade County Public Schools (MDCPS), Clean Energy Task Force, USA; and Resilience Consulting, LLC, USA.

Nancy Grimm is an affiliate of Arizona State University, USA.

Dana Hellman is an affiliate of Portland State University and CAPA Strategies, LLC, USA.

Eduardo Hinojosa-Robles is an affiliate of Instituto Municipal de Planeación Urbana, H. Ayuntamiento de Hermosillo, México.

Contributors

Jeremy S. Hoffman is an affiliate of Science Museum of Virginia and L. Douglas Wilder School of Government and Public Affairs, Virginia Commonwealth University, USA.

David M. Iwaniec is an affiliate of Georgia State University, USA.

Efrain Vizuete Jaramillo is an affiliate of Instituto Tecnológico de Sonora, Dirección de Recursos Naturales, México.

Lara Johnson is an affiliate of Urban and Community Forestry, Virginia Department of Forestry, USA.

Mandy Kuhn is an affiliate of Central Arizona Phoenix Long Term Ecological Research (CAP LTER) and School of Life Sciences, Arizona State University, USA.

Cristóbal Lamarca is an affiliate of Activa Valdivia (Consorcio Valdivia Sustentable), Chile.

Javiera Maira is an affiliate of Río Cruces Center of Wetlands (Centro de Humedales Río Cruces), Chile.

Jorge Morales-Guerrero is an affiliate of School of Sustainability, Arizona State University, USA.

Javier Navarro-Estupiñán is an affiliate of Instituto Tecnológico de Sonora, Dirección de Recursos Naturales, México.

María G. Peñúñuri is an affiliate of Instituto Municipal de Planeación Urbana, H. Ayuntamiento de Hermosillo, México.

Agustin Robles-Morúa is an affiliate of Instituto Tecnológico de Sonora, Dirección de Recursos Naturales, México.

Jason Sauer is an affiliate of Arizona State University, USA.

Alejandra Schueftan is an affiliate of Forestry Institute of Chile (Instituto Forestal de Chile), Chile.

Vivek Shandas is an affiliate of Portland State University and CAPA Strategies, LLC, USA.

Tiffany G. Troxler is an affiliate of Department of Earth and Environment, Florida International University, USA, and Sea Level Solutions Center, Institute of Environment, Florida International University, USA.

1 An introduction to researcher–practitioner partnerships for climate equity

Dana Hellman & Vivek Shandas

Current challenges

Climate change is widely considered as one of the greatest challenges to human survivorship, especially among those who have less access to and control over resources and support. Effects of a warming planet on our social fabric, economic prosperity, ecological stability, and the public's health have been areas of intensive study for decades. The extant literature largely points to several climate-induced modifiers and mechanisms that affect the lives and livelihoods of urban populations, including altered temperatures, extremes of precipitation (floods and droughts), air pollution, and infectious diseases. Extreme events, such as hurricanes, flooding, droughts, wildfires, and heat waves, are immediate and local ways that people experience climate change, and urban areas are particularly vulnerable to such events, given their location, concentration of people, and increasingly complex and interdependent infrastructures. The mounting fatalities and costs associated with extreme events are not just an indication of failures in built infrastructure, but highlight the inadequacy of institutions, resources, and information systems to prepare for and respond to extremes.

In urban areas, municipal managers, county and city councils, public agencies, and community members increasingly recognize that extant structures and past practices no longer keep urban residents out of harm's way. The 2021 'heat dome' in the Pacific Northwest was akin to a previous event of almost identical magnitude and duration that struck Chicago 26 years earlier, and yet, the fatalities and infrastructure failures point to the fact that little was learned from earlier events. Other events such as hurricanes and flooding also occur repeatedly in cities around the world, and similar patterns of adaptation inaction underscore the lack of commitment to a coordinated and informed response. With many of the most populous and fast-growing cities worldwide located along coasts, urban climate managers are rapidly exploring solutions to prevent costly and life-threatening impacts of sea level rise that are increasingly evident around the world. Yet others are located in water-scarce regions, such as the North American West, which are subject to extreme drought and heat events (Karl et al., 2009; IPCC, 2012, 2014). Compounding these vulnerabilities is the growth of the world's urban population, which the United Nations Population Program expects to double in the next generation.

The impacts of climate change are not born equally across urban populations. While urban heat is the most life threatening, floods and sea level rise arguably pose the greatest threat to built infrastructure. Evidence from around the world suggests that those who are below the poverty level, communities of color, immigrant communities, isolated, older adults, and others who have been historically marginalized are most at risk to extreme heat and consistent flooding (Reid et al., 2012; Watts et al., 2018; Voelkel et al., 2018; Chang et al., 2021). The consequences of exposure to these events are worsening, and recent studies suggest that by 2070, upward of three billion people will no longer be able to live in areas where humans have resided for the past 6,000 years (Xu et al., 2020). Even today, as much higher resolution descriptions of extreme events emerge, we observe that marginalized communities have greater exposure and, in terms of finding refuge from urban heat, are also four times as likely to be far from public health agency-sponsored cooling resources or have personal air conditioning systems (Voelkel et al., 2018). Existing studies help to define the concept of climate equity by situating race, ethnicity, and socio-economic status as key factors that disproportionately expose some urban residents to the discriminating effects of extreme events. The lack of adequate resources within these populations to mitigate or adapt to the adverse effects of a changing climate further exemplifies the importance of supporting actions that are centered in historic injustices.

Climate models and historical weather data suggest that urban communities will continue to witness increasing frequency, intensity, and duration of extreme heat in the coming decades (NOAA, 2018).

On the basis of a preponderance of evidence, practitioners face critical decisions about what strategies will be most effective for reducing exposure to and impacts from extreme climate-induced events. Arguably, those in the public sector are also responsible for safe-guarding those most vulnerable to the inequitable impacts of climate change. As costs mount, revenues waver, and calls for climate action become increasingly urgent, the need to meet competing demands can seem insurmountable for municipal managers. When evaluating expenditures on climate change versus other municipal program expenditures (e.g., public housing, schools, transit) some studies indicate woefully inadequate support for the extent of adaptation actions needed (Bachner et al., 2019). At the same time, other studies indicate that the longer municipal actions are postponed the greater the overall cost born to society. An alternative that we explore in this book is the ability for 'multi-solving' climate issues with other municipal challenges by coordinating across multiple agencies, engaging researchers, and finding opportunities to integrate climate actions into diverse and agenda-driven agency policies.

Through a series of case studies that span the Western hemisphere, this book explores the hypothesis that a coordinated response for immediate climate action requires the coming together of municipal managers and climate researchers. By integrating the emerging science about the distributional effects of climate change along with municipal policy levers for enabling actions, cities and regions can co-produce response plans that aim to ground action in science and center those communities that have the lowest amount of coping capacity. We specifically ask two questions: (1) What lessons can we find about the collaborative process from these case studies, and what findings apply specifically to climate collaborations? (2) How can integrative climate-relevant research conceivably enhance outcomes on the ground when merged with practitioner action?

The collaborative approach

The purpose of this book is not to dive deeply into the theory of collaboration, nor to extoll its perceived virtues. A robust body of literature on collaborative work – from business management to grassroots social action to public health and environmental justice – exists elsewhere, and we are writing this text from the now-common standpoint that collaboration is a promising avenue toward climate equity and resilience. However, for conceptual setup, this section includes key background details on collaborative processes generally, as well as their promise for the field of climate adaptation and resilience. Our subsequent case studies go beyond theory and potential to what we refer to as *lived collaboration*; that is, the practical manifestation of the foundational concepts discussed in this section. The contents of this book emphasize a particular variety of collaboration, which we argue is worthy of further study: that between climate researchers and practitioners.

An overview of collaboration

Existing literature on collaboration encompasses multiple varieties, including collaboration across sectors, with local communities, between governments, or between researchers and practitioners (AL-Tabbaa et al., 2014; Black et al., 2003; Nyden & Wiewel, 1992; Pavlish & Pharris, 2012; Wagner, 1997). In most cases, the underlying justification for collaboration is that siloed approaches to complex topics do not produce favorable, creative, or effective results (Coaffee & Clarke, 2015). Two (or three or four or ten) heads are better than one, so to speak, as collaborators from different backgrounds can provide unique insights and resources, while also representing potentially marginal experiences. This latter point is particularly meaningful in community-based collaborative research, wherein researchers provide community members a voice and a role in research projects that include or affect them (Harrington et al., 2019). In terms of researcher–practitioner collaboration, the end goal is typically articulated in terms of closing a gap between the two sides; reconciling functionally distinct but potentially compatible perspectives on everything from mathematics education and computer science to healthcare and social work (Bartunek, 2007; Belli, 2010).

Numerous case studies and theoretical investigations over recent decades have yielded a series of best practices and trends around collaborative partnerships. These seem to hold regardless of the industries, subjects, participants, or issues at hand. For example, collaborations work best when trust building is prioritized, allowing for the requisite time and patience; when partners have at least some shared values or goals, even if they differ on how to achieve them and when two-way communication is open and consistent (Ingold & Fischer, 2014; Pertuze et al., 2010; Tschannen-Moran, 2001). We can expect that most, if not all, of these findings will also hold within climate-specific collaborations. Indeed, with calls for urgent climate action, uncertainty around potential impacts and/or risk distributions, and a long history of disinvestment in specific urban neighborhoods, collaborative approaches will be instrumental in integrating resilience rhetoric with the lived experiences of humans facing a warming planet.

Collaborating for climate equity

An emerging body of evidence suggests that climate-induced events are discriminating and take a disproportionately heavy toll on historically marginalized communities and neighborhoods. As we encounter ever-increasing scale, intensity, and frequency of climate-induced events, we recognize that our public policies and institutional norms are failing us by exacerbating exposure to those who have limited access to coping resources. While the fields of environmental justice and social equity point to a long history of disproportionate exposure to environmental insults for Black, Indigenous, and other communities of color (BIPOC), the field of climate justice has become an increasingly important aspect of the emerging literature on collaborations, due in part to the explicit and necessary integration of biophysical and social sciences. A common feature of recent collaborative climate partnerships is the ability to advance aspects of climate resilience with and center those who may not be able to cope with the climate crisis. Whether at the global scale with the recognition about the imbalance of who is emitting the greatest amount of greenhouse gases and those hit hardest by a changing climate, or at the neighborhood scale in terms of who is experiencing the most acute impacts, the need to integrate climate equity is one of the grand challenges facing our society.

Building resilience

Building climate collaborations that focus on equity is a relatively recent phenomenon, as is the creation of researcher–practitioner collaborations for climate resilience (Campos et al., 2016; Colven & Thomson, 2018; Dey et al., 2020; Lynn, 2000; Preston et al., 2015; Wine et al., 2017). In recent years, several publications on specifically urban climate mitigation or adaptation have stated the appeal of a collaborative approach (Caughman, 2020; Hahn et al., 2020; Kern & Alber, 2009; Nagel et al., 2019). The popularity of this approach reflects what we have previously established: climate change is a challenging issue, which cannot be solved by a singular actor, discipline, or institution. Climate action not only needs sound scientific data (both environmental and social) but also depends on the implementation power of practitioners who make plans and manage programs. It is expensive and interdisciplinary, necessitating a pool of resources and expertise. Furthermore, climate equity and environmental justice require that climate researchers and practitioners alike engage with vulnerable and frontline communities and do so with recognition that some of these communities endure intergenerational trauma as a result of past research and planning practices. While researcher–practitioner collaboration is not a guarantee of community- or equity-based research, it does set the stage for such an approach. Our case studies reflect that practitioners can serve as the link between interested researchers and climate-affected populations, and some degree of community engagement regularly accompanies this kind of collaborative work. It is clear why collaboration is held up as an ideal, frequently prescribed in literature and practice and supported by theory. What remains unclear is the extent to which climate collaborations can be practically successful and why.

Notes on collaboration for this book

For the purposes of this book, we define both researchers and practitioners as encompassing a broad range of possible professional roles. Researchers are those involved in the assessment, evaluation, and characterization of climate-induced phenomena that are particular to an urban region. Many of our contributing researcher co-authors work as professors, conduct university-sponsored research projects, and are also affiliated with research laboratories within their institutions. Although the majority of researchers featured in this book are affiliated with universities, collaborators fitting this description may span other sectors. The same holds true for practitioners, who do not necessarily hail only from public agencies though again, many of those in this volume are affiliated with municipalities. The practitioner classification encompasses any individual and/or organization actively engaging in policies, plans, and/or programs directly related to local climate action. Some practitioners may have regulatory involvement, while others (e.g., non-profits, informal networks) may be directly engaging with community members and may not be providing regulatory oversight.

As noted, this book is not about promoting researcher–practitioner collaboration as a strategy for climate adaptation and resilience building; it is already widely accepted as such. Instead, we hope to bring attention to the fact that little is known – or at least, little has been written – about the dynamics of lived collaboration in the context of climate change. Unlike more straightforward targets of collaboration (e.g., business management), climate change is an immensely complex issue, touching multiple aspects of our lives, affecting an endless string of actors, and evading attempts to stop or slow it. It is a politically and culturally sensitive topic and brings with it a unique set of challenges for partners to navigate. Although there is much to learn from prior scholarship on collaborative work generally, there would be great value in understanding the dynamics of climate collaborations specifically.

Dynamics of collaborating for climate resilience

Gaps in understanding

The notion of collaborating for addressing an environmental or climate-induced challenge is not novel in itself; however, such collaborations are not typically described from a practical perspective. This makes it difficult for aspiring climate collaborators from either side to prepare for cross-sectoral work, avoid challenges and pitfalls, or gain inspiration for specific types of partnerships and outputs.

Collaboration is sometimes raised as part of a conclusion, offered as a logical next step or recommended without further explanation or instruction. Several case studies exist that detail applied and collaborative research projects on a range of germane topics, but the information they provide is variable and often missing the dimensions of the processes that enable effective climate-specific collaborations. For example, studies highlight identified drivers of effective partnership, such as having a shared belief system (Ingold & Fischer, 2014) or maintaining robust community communications (Pearce et al., 2009), yet these also emphasize the experiences of researchers, not practitioners, and fail to explore barriers as well as benefits. Even as some studies go deeper into the 'nuts and bolts' of the collaborative process (e.g., Hahn et al., 2020), there exists no comprehensive text that considers the dynamics of researcher–practitioner collaboration across case studies, provides researchers and practitioners equal opportunity to share their insights, or offers readers clear and generalizable recommendations for working in this way. In other words, collaborative processes themselves, including but not limited to their outcomes, have not been well studied or synthesized with the goal of guiding future climate collaborators.

In addition, the extant literature on the topic seems to overlook the practical dynamics of researcher–practitioner collaboration for climate resilience. For example, how are partnerships formed? How are integrative research agendas set? What is the role of applied research in a practical setting? What obstacles do partners face in navigating cross-sectoral, climate-specific collaborations, and what opportunities emerge from the same? What might we learn from communities that have actively engaged residents, researchers, and municipal managers in adapting to climate change, and are those lessons transferable? What are the means and opportunities for theory and scholarship to inform practice, and vice versa? If researchers, practitioners, and resilience advocates are to follow the advice of so many scholars and pursue a collaborative approach, functional guidance on the topic is needed. Several such collaborations are already underway, led by participants at various scales and in various sectors, as will be discussed in the next section. These offer a trove of case studies and potential contributions to a nascent knowledge base, which encompasses not only the effects of collaboration on climate action but also the lessons learned and recommendations for success. We can look to these ongoing efforts – as we have done with the case studies in this book – as a step toward typologizing, refining, and replicating researcher–practitioner collaboration for equitable urban climate resilience.

Climate collaborations in practice

As we've argued, collaborations that intentionally involve people from different professional sectors are essential for improving local and global climate adaptation efforts. Yet, such cross-sectoral partnerships, consortia, work groups, and task forces can take many forms. In some cases, community organizations invite a research entity (e.g., individual, laboratory, consulting firm) with particular content expertise, such as water treatment technology or land use planning, to contribute to a local climate action plan. In other cases, researchers invite practitioner partners to support the application of recent findings or to engage local community members. Although the initiation of the collaboration can occur through different mechanisms, the practice aims to create mutually beneficial ways to address the interrelated themes that are part of any agenda-driven effort: (1) policy development – the involvement of people with different professional knowledge in the creation of a set of rules and regulations that will govern the general public; (2) consensus building – the engagement of people who may not share the same outcome to a specific situation, yet participate in a process to achieve mutual understanding and agreement; (3) advocacy – the integration of different forms of knowledge for advancing specific aims or objectives; and (4) research and education – the use of mixed methods that often engage practitioners to support knowledge-building efforts. While generic, upon closer inspection, these forms of researcher–practitioner collaboration reveal several themes when applied to climate-relevant topics. We highlight a few notable themes in the following.

First is the notion of multiple ways of knowing, and the importance of contextualizing knowledge within the social, political, economic, cultural, racial, and gender factors that inform our ability to understand the relevance of climate change in specific locations. In the fields of climate science and analysis, past practices often lean on positivistic ideas of truth and an objective reality. The starkest examples include the biophysical-based climate models, which, since the early 1990s, shed light on the potential implications of increasing the amount of greenhouse gases in the atmosphere. Missing from several of these studies is the socially constructed nature of scientific knowledge, which is central to integrating community-based perspectives, policy agendas, and, generally, the non-research community. How might the political and social agendas vary if our existing scientific enterprise were more collaborative and engaging a non-traditional, perhaps non-scientific audience? The emergence of a pluralistic epistemology reflects the complexity of addressing this topic and the necessity to develop inclusive practices that develop plausible scientific assessments within the social factors that constitute regional and/or geopolitical differences.

Another theme that we hypothesize is central to creating enduring climate collaborations is the role of individuals and systems to span boundaries, which may, in day-to-day practices, at first glance, seem 'deviant' to institutional norms. For the purposes of this book we define 'boundary spanning' as the bringing together of individuals, objects, and practices from different fields in novel ways and to address topics that do not neatly fit into existing institutional systems. Those individuals and systems that aim to advance boundary-spanning practices must also persist long enough to identify ways that novel integration of practices can become institutionalized. Consider, for example, the creation of 'resilience officers' within municipal governments, a practice that was amplified through the Rockefeller Foundation's (now defunct) 100 Resilient Cities program. Individual agents, often funded by the foundation, were charged with integrating practices from extant municipal bureaus as a means for improving communicative practices, collaborations and, as a result, building resilience locally. Since municipal funding, or local politics, would not necessarily support boundary-spanning activities, outside funding from the foundation served to institutionalize, through individual officers, those practices that aim to support collaborations for climate resilience. The case studies throughout this compendium shed light on the specific mechanisms that allow collaborative climate partnerships to take root.

Advancing cross-sectoral collaborative partnerships seems to require a form of funding since they often occur outside of standard institutional systems of practice. Outside philanthropic sources, federal governments are increasingly seeking to improve the applicability of research outcomes by supporting interdisciplinary partnerships, though they often only include researchers within higher education. In the case of several of the chapters contained herein is the creation of the Sustainability Research Network (UREx SRN) by the US National Science Foundation. The SRN aims to 'enable synergistic and catalytic interaction among these disparate disciplines with the goal of finding answers to the most critical questions about sustainability' (NSF, 2012). In the context of this book, the UREx SRN program focused on involving researchers and practitioners that devise, analyze, and support urban infrastructure decisions in the face of climate uncertainty. Several of the authors of this compendium were involved in the UREx SRN program, and the involvement of researchers and practitioners created a place-based approach that allowed for a co-development of specific approaches, tools, and scenarios (Hamstead et al., 2021). Not all the chapters are directly related to the SRN project, though several authors will mention how this funding mechanism and involvement in the Network affected their climate collaborations.

Specific topics covered in this book

This edited book includes five case study chapters, which have at their core the common concept of researcher–practitioner collaboration. Mixed author teams, consisting of at least one researcher and one practitioner, narrate their experiences and reflect on the collaborative process. However, aside from a shared aim to collaboratively address climate change, each case study encompasses a wholly unique blend of participants, environmental stressors, geographies, justifications, theoretical underpinnings, and activities. The specific topics presented here are distinct and wide-ranging, as are collaborative efforts in the real world. Partnerships – like climate stressors, goals, and effects – vary from place to place and are accordingly viewed through different lenses, from different angles, and with different outcomes in mind. This variability further affirms the need for advanced scholarship on the types and functions of collaboration for urban climate equity and resilience.

Our five case studies provide a sampling of the possible manifestations and applications of researcher–practitioner collaboration, none of which are quite the same but all of which are effective in their own ways. These examples come from culturally and environmentally diverse locations in the United States and Latin America, illustrating that collaboration is not a rigid formula but an adaptable prescription for climate resilience in varying contexts. Case studies explicitly frame collaboration as a means of advancing climate mitigation, adaptation, or resilience efforts. The collaborative process in each case resulted directly in some identifiable outcome(s) affecting each area's climate preparedness and has also inspired future follow-up work within academic, practical, and collaborative circles. Outcomes include policies and planning guidelines, resource management strategies, and community outreach tactics, which would not have been possible outside of the collaborative structure. In fact, these cases show how partnerships enabled disparate entities to integrate, achieve mutual benefits, and overcome common barriers such as insufficient access to funding, interdisciplinary expertise, or community resources and knowledge at the individual level. Table 1.1. summarizes the key elements of the case study chapters

Organization of the book and objectives

Chapters 2 through 6 represent five case studies from locations across the United States and Latin America. These chapters follow a standardized

An introduction to researcher–practitioner partnerships 11

Table 1.1 Overview of the content presented in each chapter.

Case Study Location	Topic	Target Stressor(s)	Types of Partner Institutions	Conceptual Basis	Methods/ Activities	Outcomes
Phoenix, Arizona	Urban greenspace as a multi-functional resilience solution	Heat; flooding; poor health outcomes	University; research institution; elementary school	Nature-based solutions; environmental justice	Photovoice; designing future scenarios; storyboarding	Youth-designed future visions; introduction of an empowerment and abundance framework for climate-affected communities; connection of past to present to future environmental conditions; micro-local data
Valdivia, Chile	Balancing urban development with stormwater management and wetland conservation	Pluvial flooding	University; research institution; government agency; non-governmental organization; environmental organization	Social-Ecological-Technological Systems (SETS)	Scenarios workshops; working group meetings	New urban development paradigm focused on nature-based solutions that has been put into practice for several projects; pilot projects of wastewater-purifying wetlands; National Wetland Protection Law; novel research directions
Miami, Florida	Creating a multi-functional, regional resilience strategy backed by policy	Sea level rise; flooding; heat	University; government agency; private business	Interacting stressors and solutions; general resilience	Citizen science data collection; governance survey; scenarios workshops	Increased public outreach and awareness; practical learning opportunities; novel resilience metrics; cost-saving measures and new funding sources; decision-making tools for governments; hyper-local data

(Continued)

Table 1.1 (Continued)

Case Study Location	Topic	Target Stressor(s)	Types of Partner Institutions	Conceptual Basis	Methods/ Activities	Outcomes
Hermosillo, Mexico	Green infrastructure as a multi-functional resilience solution	Air quality; heat; flooding	University; government agency	Nature-based solutions	Scenarios workshops; scientific (physical) data collection; planning studies; spatial analysis and modeling; feasibility mapping	Changes to policy and urban development guidelines; identification of priority sites for green infrastructure
Richmond, Virginia	Framework for engaging the public in climate data collection and solutions	Heat	Science museum; university; government agency	Community science; participatory action research	Heat island mapping (conducted by community volunteers)	Novel engagement framework for practitioners; hyper-local data; localized heat vulnerability index; new partnerships and funding sources

An introduction to researcher–practitioner partnerships 13

format, allowing for easier comparison and synthesis across cases. The common sections to be found in each case study chapter are as follows:

- Introduction.
- Description of the case study area: spatial and demographic profile of the city; overview of relevant institutions, politics, policies; major climate concerns and past problems.
- Rationale for doing this work: both academic and practical/applied goals or contributions.
- Details of what was done: how collaboration began and who participated; descriptions of specific activities, research questions, and methods.
- Outcomes: practical and academic outcomes of the work to date; ongoing partnership potential; strengths and weaknesses of the process.

Additionally, contributing authors respond to a standard set of questions in a Reflections section at the end of each chapter:

- What obstacles did you encounter when working across sectors? (*Barriers and obstacles*)
- What worked well, or what benefits did you see? (*Benefits and enablers*)
- What recommendations or advice would you give to others working in this way? (*Recommendations and advice*)
- What do you envision to be the future of the work you created? (*Next steps for this work*)

Chapter 7 provides a synthesis of the information presented in case study chapters. This includes common themes; findings that appear particularly relevant for the field of climate resilience; the observed benefits of collaboration for climate action on the ground; and recommendations for next steps. We will specifically discuss these findings as they relate to potential future directions of researcher–practitioner collaboration for equitable climate mitigation, adaptation, and resilience planning.

By building an empirical knowledge base around researcher–practitioner collaboration, and engaging individuals with varying perspectives and knowledge, this book will provide guidance to those working collaboratively toward urban climate change resilience, now and in the future. The content presented here is meant to (1) frame the topic of researcher–practitioner collaboration for climate resilience and equity as deserving further study, given that it is conceptually popular and urgently important yet not well understood on a functional level; (2) begin to build a cohesive base of evidence and narratives on the subject as a starting point for future investigation; and (3) provide preliminary guidance on the facets of researcher–practitioner collaboration, which are seemingly typical of collaborations in general, as well as those which are unique to the field of climate resilience. While these are useful starting points, there are other important considerations that will not be covered herein. This book does not identify which urban areas will require greater or lesser resources to safeguard; the specific policies or programs that will enable success across all urban areas; or a transferable means of weighing the importance of different climate-induced stressors in different contexts. Rather, our case studies rely on personal testimonies about the effectiveness of researcher–practitioner collaborations as a procedural approach to improve the management of cities among an ever-increasing set of climate-induced hazards. It is our hope that this work will pique the interest of scholars and practitioners alike, and encourage deeper inquiry into the dynamics and observable benefits of climate collaboration. This may lead to a clear suite of recommendations, best practices, and collaborative strategies that can be applied to partnerships in a variety of social, political, and environmental contexts, enhancing our collective capacity to build climate resilience together.

References

AL-Tabbaa, O., Leach, D., & March, J. (2014). Collaboration between nonprofit and business sectors: A framework to guide strategy development for nonprofit organizations. *VOLUNTAS: International Journal of Voluntary and Nonprofit Organizations, 25*(3), 657–678. https://doi.org/10.1007/s11266-013-9357-6

Bachner, G., Bednar-Friedl, B., & Knittel, N. (2019). How does climate change adaptation affect public budgets? Development of an assessment framework and a demonstration for Austria. *Mitig Adapt Strateg Glob Change, 24*, 1325–1341. https://doi.org/10.1007/s11027-019-9842-3

Bartunek, J. M. (2007). Academic-practitioner collaboration need not require joint or relevant research: Toward a relational scholarship of integration. *Academy of Management Journal, 50*(6), 1323–1333. https://doi.org/10.5465/amj.2007.28165912

Belli, G. (2010). Bridging the researcher-practitioner gap: Views from different fields. *8th International Conference on Teaching Statistics Invited Paper.* Retrieved from http://citeseerx.ist.psu.edu/viewdoc/download?doi=10.1.1.205.1151&rep=rep1&type

Black, L. J., Cresswell, A. M., Luna, L. F., Pardo, T. A., Martinez, I. J., Thompson, F., . . . Cook, M. (2003). A dynamic theory of collaboration: A structural approach to facilitating intergovernmental use of information technology. *36th Annual Hawaii International Conference on System Sciences, 2003: Proceedings of the*, IEEE, Big Island, HI, USA (12 pp). https://doi.org/10.1109/HICSS.2003.1174222

Campos, I., Vizinho, A., Coelho, C., Alves, F., Truninger, M., Pereira, C., . . . Penha Lopes, G. (2016). Participation, scenarios and pathways in long-term planning for climate change adaptation. *Planning Theory & Practice, 17*(4), 537–556. https://doi.org/10.1080/14649357.2016.1215511

Caughman, L. E. (2020). *Collaboration and evaluation in urban sustainability and resilience transformations: The keys to a just transition?* (Doctoral dissertation), Portland, OR: Portland State University.

Chang, H., Pallathadka, A., Sauer, J., Grimm, N. B., Zimmerman, R., Cheng, C., . . . & Herreros-Cantis, P. (2021). Assessment of urban flood vulnerability using the social-ecological-technological systems framework in six US cities. *Sustainable Cities and Society, 68*, 102786. https://doi.org/10.1016/j.scs.2021.102786

Coaffee, J., & Clarke, J. (2015). On securing the generational challenge of urban resilience. *Town Planning Review, 86*(3), 249–255. https://doi.org/10.3828/tpr.2015.16

Colven, E., & Thomson, M. J. (2018). Bridging the divide between human and physical geography: Potential avenues for collaborative research on climate modeling. *Geography Compass, 13*(2), e12418. https://doi.org/10.1111/gec3.12418

Dey, C. J., Rego, A. I., Midwood, J. D., & Koops, M. A. (2020). A review and meta-analysis of collaborative research prioritization studies in ecology, biodiversity conservation and environmental science. *Proceedings of the Royal Society B: Biological Sciences, 287*(1923), 20200012. https://doi.org/10.1098/rspb.2020.0012

Hahn, M. B., Kemp, C., Ward-Waller, C., Donovan, S., Schmidt, J. I., & Bauer, S. (2020). Collaborative climate mitigation and adaptation planning with university, community, and municipal partners: A case study in Anchorage, Alaska. *Local Environment, 25*(9), 648–665. https://doi.org/10.1080/13549839.2020.1811655

Hamstead, Z., Iwaniec, D. M., McPhearson, P. T., Berbés-Blázquez, M., Cook, E. M., & Munoz-Erickson, T. A. (Eds.). (2021). *Resilent urban futures*. Cham, Switzerland: Springer. ISBN: 978-3-030-63130-7

Harrington, C., Erete, S., & Piper, A. M. (2019). Deconstructing community-based collaborative design: Towards more equitable participatory design engagements. *Proceedings of the ACM on Human-Computer Interaction, 3*(CSCW), 1–25. https://doi.org/10.1145/3359318

Ingold, K., & Fischer, M. (2014). Drivers of collaboration to mitigate climate change: An illustration of Swiss climate policy over 15 years. *Global Environmental Change, 24*, 88–98. https://doi.org/10.1016/j.gloenvcha.2013.11.021

IPCC (2012). C.B. Field, V. Barros, T.F. Stocker, D. Qin, D.J. Dokken, K.L. Ebi, M.D. Mastrandrea, K.J. Mach, G.-K. Plattner, S.K. Allen, M. Tignor, & P.M. Midgley (Eds.) Cambridge University Press, Cambridge, UK.

IPCC (2014). *Climate Change 2014: Synthesis Report.* Contribution of Working Groups I, II and III to the Fifth Assessment Report of the Intergovernmental Panel on Climate Change [Core Writing Team, R.K. Pachauri and L.A. Meyer (Eds.)]. IPCC, Geneva, Switzerland.

Karl, T.R., Melillo, J.M., & Peterson, T.C. (Eds.) (2009). *Global climate change impacts in the United States.* Cambridge Univ. Press, Cambridge, UK.

Kern, K., & Alber, G. (2009, October 9–10). Governing climate change in cities: Modes of urban climate governance in multi-level systems. *The International Conference on Competitive Cities and Climate Change*, Milan, Italy (pp. 171–196).

Lynn, F. M. (2000). Community-scientist collaboration in environmental research. *American Behavioral Scientist, 44*(4), 649–663. https://doi.org/10.1177/00027640021956305

Nagel, M., Stark, M., Satoh, K., Schmitt, M., & Kaip, E. (2019). Diversity in collaboration: Networks in urban climate change governance. *Urban Climate, 29*, 100502. https://doi.org/10.1016/j.uclim.2019.100502

NOAA (2018). *NOAA National Centers for Environmental Information, State of the Climate: Global Climate Report for Annual 2018.* Retrieved from https://www.ncdc.noaa.gov/sotc/global/201813

NSF (2012). *Two NSF Sustainability Research Networks Are Each Awarded $12 Million*. Retrieved from https://www.nsf.gov/news/news_summ.jsp?cntn_id=125599

Nyden, P., & Wiewel, W. (1992). Collaborative research: Harnessing the tensions between researcher and practitioner. *The American Sociologist*, *23*(4), 43–55. https://doi.org/10.1007/BF02691930

Pavlish, C. P., & Pharris, M. D. (2012). *Community-based collaborative action research: A nursing approach*. Sudbury, MA: Jones & Bartlett Learning.

Pearce, T. D., Ford, J. D., Laidler, G. J., Smit, B., Duerden, F., Allarut, M., . . . Wandel, J. (2009). Community collaboration and climate change research in the Canadian Arctic. *Polar Research*, *28*(1), 10–27. https://doi.org/10.1111/j.1751-8369.2008.00094.x

Pertuze, J. A., Calder, E. S., Greitzer, E. M., & Lucas, W. A. (2010). Best practices for industry-university collaboration. *MIT Sloan Management Review, Summer 2010 Research Feature*. Retrieved from https://sloanreview.mit.edu/article/best-practices-for-industry-university-collaboration/

Preston, B. L., Rickards, L., Fünfgeld, H., & Keenan, R. J. (2015). Toward reflexive climate adaptation research. *Current Opinion in Environmental Sustainability*, *14*, 127–135. https://doi.org/10.1016/j.cosust.2015.05.002

Reid, C. E., Mann, J. K., Alfasso, R., English, P. B., King, G. C., Lincoln, R. A., … Balmes, J. R. (2012). Evaluation of a heat vulnerability index on abnormally hot days: An environmental public health tracking study. *Environmental Health Perspectives*, *120*(5), 715–720. https://doi.org/10.1289/ehp.1103766

Tschannen-Moran, M. (2001). Collaboration and the need for trust. *Journal of Educational Administration*, *39*(4), 308–331. https://doi.org/10.1108/EUM0000000005493

Voelkel, J., Hellman, D., Sakuma, R., & Shandas, V. (2018). Assessing vulnerability to urban heat: A study of disproportionate heat exposure and access to refuge by socio-demographic status in Portland, Oregon. *International Journal of Environmental Research and Public Health*, *15*(4), 640. https://doi.org/10.3390/ijerph15040640

Wagner, J. (1997). The unavoidable intervention of educational research: A framework for reconsidering researcher-practitioner cooperation. *Educational Researcher*, *26*(7), 13–22. https://doi.org/10.3102/0013189X026007013

Watts, N., Amann, M., Arnell, N., Ayeb-Karlsson, S., Belesova, K., Berry, H., ... & Costello, A. (2018). The 2018 report of the Lancet Countdown on health and climate change: shaping the health of nations for centuries to come. *The Lancet*, *392*(10163), 2479–2514.

Wine, O., Ambrose, S., Campbell, S., Villeneuve, P. J., Burns, K. K., & Vargas, A. O. (2017). Key components of collaborative research in the context of environmental health: A scoping review. *Journal of Research Practice*, *13*(2). Retrieved from https://eric.ed.gov/?id=EJ1174006

Xu, H., Kohler, T. A., Lenton, T. M., Svenning, J.-C., & Scheffer, M. (2020). Future of the human climate niche C. *Proceedings of the National Academy of Sciences*, *117*(21), 11350–11355.

2 Designing urban greenspace from the grassroots up

The '*barrio* innovation' approach

Marta Berbés-Blázquez, Vanya Bisht, Regional Carrillo, Monique Franco, Mandy Kuhn & Jorge Morales-Guerrero

Introduction

For the past decade, cities have been looking to nature-based solutions as a way to combat environmental issues that impact the quality of life of city dwellers. The turn toward greening cities builds on a longer tradition of ideas in urban planning of designing *with* nature (after McHarg, 1969; Hough, 2004) and the more recent recognition that urban ecosystem services provide multiple benefits simultaneously, such as pleasing aesthetics, climate regulation, educational and recreational opportunities, carbon sequestration, and food, to name a few (Gómez-Baggethun et al., 2013; McPhearson et al., 2014). With both climate change and urbanization intensifying in the coming decades, which forecasts more frequent and more severe heat waves and flood events in cities (IPCC, 2021), green infrastructure is seen as being able to reduce the impact of climate extremes, while also promoting healthy lifestyles, and guide overall community and infrastructure development (Birch & Wachter, 2008).

While the benefits of nature-based solutions are clear, urban greenspaces – from city parks to gardens to naturalized areas such as wetlands – are unevenly distributed in cities. In a pattern that repeats itself throughout many cities in North America, more affluent parts of cities tend to enjoy higher access to greenspace benefits (Heynen et al., 2006). Conversely, the presence of environmental disamenities, such as air pollution, soil contamination, or frequent flooding, tends to coincide with areas inhabited by low-income and minoritized populations. In the city of Phoenix, AZ, where our work is located, these patterns of environmental injustice have been clearly documented (Bolin et al., 2000; Boucher et al., 2021). Starting with the erasure of the Indigenous presence from the land, followed by decades of spatially segregated growth and redlining in the 1930s, Hispanic and African American populations have been historically relegated to the South and West of Phoenix, which have lagged behind in

DOI: 10.4324/9781003208723-2

infrastructure and investment compared to the more affluent and whiter parts of town (Bolin et al., 2005; York et al., 2014). This is reflected in differences in the urban heat island effect, which is more pronounced in low-income neighborhoods (Connors et al., 2013), along with the presence of industrial zoning (Boucher et al., 2021), or higher concentrations of particulate matter PM 2.5 in the air (Pope et al., 2016).

Greening efforts in cities can advance environmental justice goals (Rubin, 2008). Environmental justice emerged during the 1970s and 1980s in the United States at the confluence of the environmental, civil rights, and labor movements. Although the location of waste sites near African American populations was a catalytic moment in the history of environmental justice, its scope has broadened to shape debates on other aspects of urban development, such as public transit and energy transitions (Schlosberg & Collins, 2014). Environmental justice is usually conceived as encompassing distributional, procedural, and recognitional aspects of justice (Fraser, 2000; Young, 1990; Schlosberg, 2007). Distributional justice has to do with the documentation of spatial patterns of environmental amenities and disamenities and how these patterns correspond to socio-demographic characteristics. For example, the aforementioned work documenting how the location of waste treatment facilities in the United States corresponds to the location of communities of color emphasizes distributional injustices (Bullard, 1994, 2000). On the other hand, procedural justice focuses on the process of environmental decision-making, how it is organized, and who is included and excluded from participating. From large issues of voter suppression to small details such as the scheduling of consultation meetings, these are all aspects of procedural justice. Last, recognitional justice has to do with the respectful treatment of difference, especially of culturally or historically distinct groups, such as Indigenous peoples, in processes of decision-making.

This chapter presents a collaboration between graduate students from Arizona State University (ASU) (Bisht [School for the Future of Innovation in Society], Morales-Guerrero [School of Sustainability], and Kuhn [School of Life Sciences]); researchers from the Central Arizona-Phoenix Long-Term Ecological Research (CAP LTER) program (Berbés-Blázquez and Franco); and a teacher from Academia del Pueblo (Carrillo), a middle school in Phoenix that serves a majority of Latinx and low-income students. Our collaboration was anchored in environmental justice and it sought to explore urban greenspace from the perspective of Latinx youth. Although our work ultimately seeks to increase the benefits that urban youth experience from greenspace, and thus has a component of distributional justice, it was designed with the procedural and recognitional aspects of justice in mind. That is, the impetus of the work was to model a process that would stay with the youth and that centered not only their voices but their culture. We use the term '*barrio* innovation' to refer to our approach, which is based on design thinking but rooted in and driven by community.

Description of the case study area

Situated in the heart of the Sonoran desert, the Phoenix Metropolitan Area is the sixth largest city in the United States and home to nearly five million residents. The city is spatially segregated with minoritized and low-income populations living predominantly in the South and West areas of Phoenix. Climate change in the Southwest will lead to increased temperatures, continued drought, more frequent and more severe floods, and increased risk of wildfires (Garfin et al., 2013; USGCRP, 2017). Many of these impacts are already being felt by Phoenicians. For example, excessive heat during the summer months regularly results in hospitalizations, and in the summer of 2020, Maricopa County reported 323 heat-associated deaths (Maricopa County Public Health, 2020). As well, the Southwest region is currently experiencing a 20-year drought, due to lower winter–spring precipitation that impacts the water supply, as well as the decline of snowpack at higher elevations that supports flow in major water-supply rivers (USGCRP, 2017). In the summer of 2021, the federal government declared a water shortage on the Colorado River as water levels in Lake Mead and Lake Powell reservoirs fell to nearly a third of their capacity, prompting water cuts for Arizona farmers in 2022.

Despite the clear risk that climate change poses for the region, Maricopa County, where Phoenix is located, continues to be one of the fastest-growing counties in the United States, which adds urgency to the need to adapt to climate change impacts. Among the sustainability commitments of the City of Phoenix is the *Tree & Shade Master Plan* (2010), which lays down a vision for increasing urban tree canopy from the current 11%–13% to 25% by 2030, using native species, which will reduce urban heat island effect and improve walkability. As well, Phoenix joined the C40 network in 2020, a network of cities around the world committed to share knowledge to reduce the impacts of climate change and improve air quality. The C40 network aims to halve carbon emissions within the decade. Related to their C40 commitment, Phoenix is currently drafting its first Climate Action Plan, which was presented to the council in October 2021. Expanding and preserving greenspace is a key part of all the aforementioned sustainability initiatives in Phoenix. Trees, grassy areas, and gardens are all seen as providing important cooling benefits that reduce the urban heat island effect (Nelson et al., 2021; Zhang et al., 2017), in addition to offering other benefits for human health and well-being. Hence, there is an opportunity in planning for climate resilience to also deliver a more equitable distribution of ecosystem benefits across the city.

Our project approached the exploration of greenspace from a perspective rooted in environmental justice. Academia del Pueblo is a Title 1, K-8th grade elementary school serving a mostly Latinx population of 400 students. Academia del Pueblo's mission is 'to serve the academic, social and individual needs of students by developing community-based bilingual and multicultural educational programs that enhance student knowledge and skills to prepare them to successfully respond to the social, economic, scientific and technological challenges in our society.' Academia del Pueblo has a strong belief in the benefits of project-based learning as an educational tool that provides an engaging learning experience for students while providing the opportunity for students to dive into the issues endemic to their own communities. We worked with two middle school classes of 13- and 14-year-old students attending the eighth grade. Academia del Pueblo is situated in Central City Phoenix, which is a historical neighborhood that includes not only the vibrant downtown core but also the international airport and a significant proportion of land dedicated to heavy industries (e.g., cement, auto and parts industry, recycling and waste management). The school itself backs onto the I-17 highway, and it is surrounded by industrial, commercial, and low-density residential areas. There are two smaller public parks within a mile (~20-minute walk) from Academia del Pueblo, although tree cover is generally low in the area surrounding the school and in the parks themselves. In addition, the school is in close proximity to the local Rio Salado Habitat Restoration area and the Nina Mason Pulliam Rio Salado Audubon Center. Both of these natural spaces are difficult to access from the school by foot, but they do offer opportunities to explore the desert landscape, including rare desert wetlands, and they have educational programming.

While increasing the amount of greenspace in the neighborhood would be beneficial for local cooling and general enjoyment, our project wanted to approach greenspace beyond distributional considerations. That is, we started from the premise that those who are closer to an issue are also closer to the solution. We understood that greenspace may not be universally desirable, or at least, that not everyone is equally capable of deriving the same benefits from urban parks. For example, experience tells us that teenagers, families, and elders use public parks in very different ways. Women have different perceptions than men of what constitutes safety around natural and secluded areas. Communities have cultural preferences for the sports that they practice outdoors, for example, baseball versus cricket versus tai chi. Garden aesthetics and uses vary across cultural groups. The very question of who a park serves – Only humans? Pollinators? Coyotes? – does not have a single answer. Thus, the uses that people make out of greenspace are shaped by a variety of factors such as age, gender, and ethnicity. From this perspective, we understood our work not as a prescription but as an exploration of the meanings of greenspace for urban youth and their vision for the community in which they are growing up.

Rationale for doing this work

Our work occurred in the context of the classroom. Our approach to working with the students was anchored in theories of environmental justice but practically oriented toward participatory action research, or PAR, (Cornwall & Jewkes, 1995) and popular education (Freire, 1996). PAR emerged in development practice in the 1980s, and popular education has a long tradition in Latin America, especially since the 1970s. Both of these approaches center engagement as a vehicle for learning and discovery. What this means is that we sought to model an approach to inquiry that centered the students not as passive receivers of knowledge but as active co-creators and equal participants. In this way, these approaches also challenge traditional power structures that dictate that students should learn from their teachers, and instead we facilitated a process of self-discovery. As such, our group took the role of catalysts, rather than leaders when we were in the classroom. On this note, it was important to reflect on our own positionalities in this process: Berbés-Blázquez is a cisgender, Hispanic immigrant woman, and a settler. Bisht is an international student of Indian origin. Carrillo is a queer Mexican-American cisgender male. Franco is multi-racial and native to Phoenix. Kuhn is a cisgender white woman of American and Caribbean descent. Morales-Guerrero is cisgender, *chabochi* (Ralámuli word for mixed-heritage person with Indigenous and European descent), Mexican, and queer. Thus, we occupied different spaces in the insider–outsider spectrum, and it was important to keep our positionalities in mind when interacting with the students.

PAR and popular education have traditionally been used in the context of struggle. The approaches are thus oriented toward praxis, which is about the implementation of theory into action. We did this by emphasizing how knowledge needed to be mobilized beyond the classroom walls. Our intention was to model a process that allowed students to name their realities, envision alternative futures, and feel empowered to act on them. This is why the project was connected from the start to local environmental justice organizations (Chispa Arizona) and arts and culture organizations (The Sagrado Galleria) so that students could understand the work that organizers do and the tools they use.

Details of what was done

All projects have an origin story, so here is ours (see also Figure 2.1). All of the authors in this chapter, except Carrillo, are associated with Arizona State University, where we share research interests on sustainability science and equity. In addition, Berbés-Blázquez, Bisht, Franco, and Kuhn have connections with the CAP LTER group that is housed at the university. The CAP LTER brings together approximately 100 researchers and graduate students across the campus, and it is one of the two urban sites of the LTER network, funded through the National Science Foundation. The CAP LTER was launched in 1997 with the purpose of studying urban ecology from a broad, interdisciplinary lens. The main research activities of the CAP LTER are to collect longitudinal data on key ecological indicators in the Phoenix valley, for example, species counts, biogeochemical cycles, wetland dynamics; however, it increasingly supports social-ecological and social science research (Pickett et al., 2016). Indeed, there is a small but growing portion of CAP LTER's research portfolio that involves working with decision-makers and an even smaller part that works with residents in participatory ways. Importantly, CAP LTER has a program manager for education and outreach who liaises with schools and teachers to support the creation of activities and curriculum for K-12 education. Franco was hired for this position in 2020.

All of the authors are connected in different ways to activist circles in Phoenix in the domains of environmental justice, LGBTQ rights, anti-racism, food insecurity, and migrant rights. These connections are not professional but rather as volunteers, co-organizers, learners, and allies. It was one of the environmental justice organizations, Chispa Arizona, which initially put Berbés-Blázquez, Morales-Guerrero, and Carrillo in touch with the idea of developing school activities to raise environmental awareness in Carrillo's social science class. The subsequent focus on greenspace emerged to match a developing public campaign about protecting public lands led by Chispa. In addition, there were two large development projects occurring in the area near Academia del Pueblo School that provided a backdrop for our work. One was the extension of the light-rail train from downtown Phoenix into South Phoenix, and the other one was the Rio Reimagined project, which will restore the flow to the Salt River. Both of these initiatives are controversial because they will bring green amenities and transit to an underserved area of Phoenix, but they will also presumably lead to the gentrification of the community. Thus, opening up the conversation with the students about urban planning and greenspace seemed opportune.

We are currently starting our third year of the project. Both the 2019–2020 and the 2020–2021 school years were impacted by the coronavirus

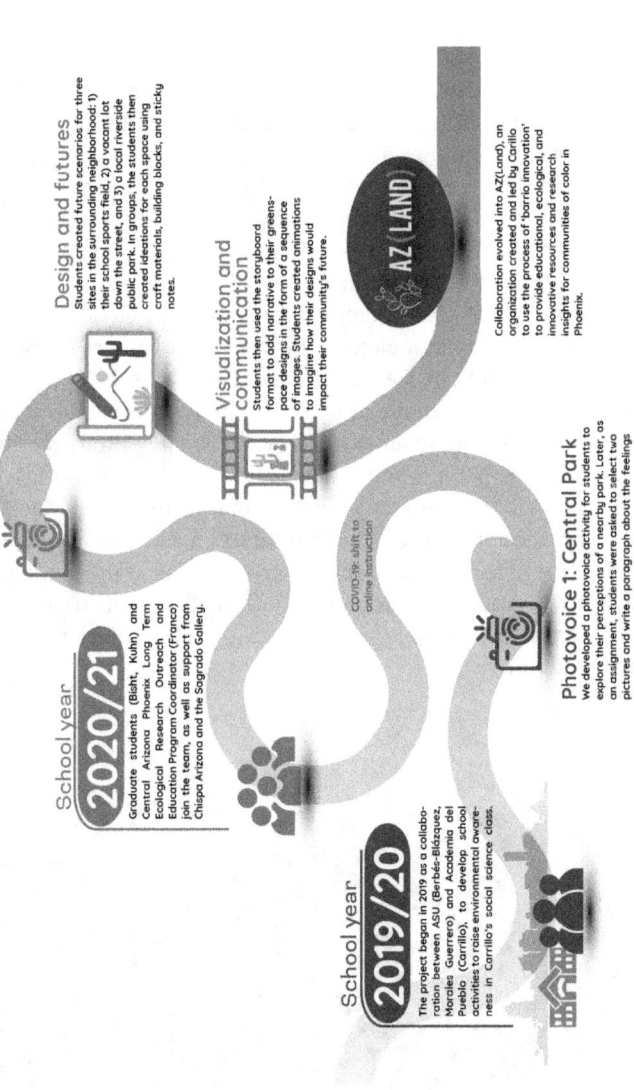

Figure 2.1 The ebb and flow of activities and people associated with our collaborative project.

pandemic that led to a school lockdown that began in March 2020 and lasted until March 2021. In Figure 2.1, we outline the specific activities that we conducted with the students in chronological order.

2019–2020 school year

This project began in 2019 as a collaboration between ASU (Berbés-Blázquez, Morales-Guerrero) and Academia del Pueblo (Carrillo). In the first year of the project, we designed a photovoice activity for the students to explore their perceptions of a nearby park. We brought the class to Central Park in Phoenix and encouraged them to walk around and take pictures (Figure 2.2). Later, as an assignment, students were asked to select two pictures and write a paragraph about the feelings that those images elicited for them. Students were asked to write about both positive and negative feelings associated with the park. The preliminary analysis of the images and text by Berbés-Blázquez and Morales-Guerrero showed that the park elicited a range of emotions in the students. In general, they found the park lacking in amenities for them. They pointed to the basketball court and the playground (at the time under construction) as positive features, but there were many photographs showing the lack of shade, benches, or trees, which led to a feeling of ennui. Unfortunately, right as we were starting to share the preliminary analysis of the photographs with the students, the coronavirus pandemic forced schools to lock down, and the project was put on hold, as all educational institutions scrambled to finish the school year.

Figure 2.2 Pictures taken by Academia del Pueblo students during their visit to Central Park, Phoenix, in January 2020.

2020–2021 school year

We resumed activities in the 2020–2021 school year while Academia del Pueblo had switched to online instruction. At this time, graduate students (Bisht, Kuhn) and CAP LTER Outreach and Education Program Coordinator (Franco) joined the original team. In addition, we had support from Chispa Arizona, a Latinx environmental justice organization that is active in the valley, and The Sagrado Galleria, a community arts organization and art gallery in South Phoenix. In 2020–2021 we kept the photovoice exercise from the previous year as a way of identifying and naming the youth's realities, but we added a visioning component that used the principles of design thinking to imagine positive futures.

Photovoice

The photovoice assignment maintained the same basic structure. However, since students were not attending school in person, we simply asked them to take pictures of greenspace around their neighborhood. We left the instructions purposely vague to encourage them to find nature in the city without preconceptions. This revealed a broader understanding of the types of nature to which the students had access, which can be grouped into five main types of experiences. First, public parks remained important ways in which students experienced nature. Overwhelmingly, parks were associated with positive and peaceful feelings, akin to urban oases. Second, students took pictures of what we called 'pass-by nature,' which included the naturalized spaces near roadways, in parking lots, or surrounding large buildings, typically taken during a car or bus ride. Students showed indifference to this type of nature. The third type of nature that students photographed was the nature in their neighborhood, which usually comprised shots of street trees and alleyways. The comments were often critical of the aesthetics of their streetscape, for example, the lack of large trees, but also of the state of grey infrastructure, for example, pavement in poor condition or the lack of sidewalks. The fourth type of nature was nature in their homes. Many students photographed their yards or the view from their homes. This was a particularly revealing set of pictures since they often reflected a sense of pride in showing their space but also their concerns for their neighborhood, for example, safety issues. Last, a few pictures depicted what we called 'big nature.' These were landscape pictures, such as sunsets or views of the South Mountain. Although it was a small set, these pictures revealed strong positive feelings toward outdoor experiences. The full set of pictures was presented to the students to reflect on the range of uses and emotions that urban nature offered to them currently and use this as a departing point for thinking about how they imagine the future of urban greenspace in their community.

Design and futures

After presenting to the students the assessment of their photos, we introduced the idea of design. Design was presented to them by The Sagrado Galleria as a way of participating in the decision-making processes and intervening in the future of their community. Students created future scenarios for three sites in the surrounding neighborhood: (1) their school sports field, (2) a vacant lot down the street, and (3) a local riverside public park (Figure 2.3). Students were provided the satellite images of each site and encouraged to brainstorm how they would transform each space. In groups, the students created ideations for each space using craft materials, building blocks, and sticky notes. Students had opportunities to reflect and revise their designs throughout this phase as they learned about local ecosystem services from a scientific and a traditional ecological knowledge perspective. These activities included explorations of (1) native plant life adaptations and water access, (2) the traditional uses of native plants and water by Indigenous people in the area, and (3) differences in surface temperatures of different materials using infrared thermometers and thermal imaging and mapping tools to compare their community with neighboring communities.

Figure 2.3 Left: Students brainstorming future visions for a local riverside park. Right: Students' design to transform a local vacant lot into a food truck park and greenspace.

Visualization and communication

The last activity of the greenspace project was meant to enable students to visualize a story about the future they wanted to see for their community. We used the storyboard format to visualize the narrative in the form of a sequence of images, or concept drawings, that can later be combined to create a motion film or video (Hart, 2013). These stories loosely incorporated structural elements of characters, objects, settings, and events, based on the previous activities carried out in the class (Stackelberg, 2011). We asked the students to come up with characters that resembled people in their community, while the transformed spaces designed in the previous activity provided a setting for the story. We did not provide a structure for the sequence of events in the story, but many students on their own wrote stories describing a process of change that created a better environment or socio-economic conditions in their community. For example, there are stories where community members come together to clean city parks, place solar panels over buildings, shut down a polluting factory, or buy food for a homeless person (Figure 2.4). We recorded the voices of students for each of the scenes of the storyboard, playing the characters they had created and speaking the dialogues they had written. These audio recordings, along with the images of the storyboards, were used to create videos for each of the stories.

As we move to prepare for the third year of this project, we want to maintain a similar overall structure with activities that allow students to name

Figure 2.4 Storyboard created by students from Academia del Pueblo on 'bringing a change.'

their experiences and envision better futures. However, there are exciting possibilities to add a component of communication and advocacy. Thus we are pursuing partnerships with community organizers and local policy-makers so that the students have a chance to express their vision for change to the wider community and politicians in city hall.

Outcomes

Our goal with this project has been to plant seeds in the minds of the youth so that they can be agents of change in their communities. Like seeds, it is hard to know where and which ones will find fertile ground to grow. However, we believe that the main outcome emerging from our work is an approach we have chosen to call '*barrio* innovation' that is guiding the creation of a community grassroots organization AZ(Land) led by Carrillo and Franco. The purpose of AZ(Land) is to offer the '*barrio* innovation' approach beyond the classroom to tackle environmental issues affecting the community more broadly. The way we see it, the '*barrio* innovation' has the following elements:

1. *A mind frame of abundance.* Barrio innovation embraces a mind frame of abundance by recognizing the inherent strength of the groups with whom we work. It is thus an asset-based approach (Mathie & Cunningham, 2003), which recognizes that communities know and have always known. This is why all of our activities were designed to provide minimal structure that centered the voices of the students and not our own. For example, through photovoice or storyboarding, the students present their realities as they see them, the students choose what they want to portray. Oftentimes the pictures or stories revealed a rich, textured, and complex reality that showed the students' concerns but, more importantly, the sources of strength as well. A corollary of the abundance mindset is that it validates students' knowledge and experiences as the students are reminded that they are experts about life in their community and that the answer to the issues lies within them.
2. *A focus on pathways.* The '*barrio* innovation' approach seeks to demonstrate the ties between the past, the present, and the future of the community. We look at the past as an analytical tool to interpret the historical and layered nature of present-day injustices. For instance, we talk about zoning as a key mechanism that has shaped the spatial distribution of environmental amenities in the city so that students understand that they have received a legacy of racist practices but also, that they can influence present-day decisions that will shape their future. Both the visioning exercise and the storyboarding push the students

to develop their vision for a desirable future. We use visions as important catalysts for change because they inspire hope. As well, the gap between what is, in the present, and what should be, in the vision, questions what and why we take for granted our current conditions. Thus, the focus on the connection between past, present, and future helps us to maintain the emphasis on the possibility for transformation.

3. *A focus on the micro-local.* Like the *barrio* ('neighborhood'), our approach is tied to place and is micro-local in scale. This responds to the need to create genuine and reciprocal relationships. Working within the context of a classroom means that we are building on student–teacher relationships, which is one of the most important bonds that students form during their childhood. Most of the students have known Carrillo for several years, and that level of trust is reflected in how the students engaged with the different research activities. In addition, the focus on the micro-local centers the importance of the cultural context. Phoenix is a diverse city, and historical neighborhoods such as Central City have their own identity that needs to be understood in order to function in that space. For example, during the round of photovoice in the 2019–2020 school year, students took many pictures of the chain-link fence that surrounds Central Park. The majority of the students talked about the aesthetics of the fence in negative terms, comparing it to a prison. It was only after talking to old-timers in the community that we understood that neighbors had rallied decades earlier to erect the fence in order to keep drug activity out of the park and provide a safe space for youth. Finally, the rootedness of the approach also allows us to think historically about the knowledge that lives and belongs in places. For many groups that are currently disenfranchised, learning about this knowledge can be a source of pride and connection to culture and identity.

Reflections

Barriers and obstacles

One of the challenges that are often overlooked in collaborations is that coordinating a self-organized group is difficult. In our case, every team member had other responsibilities besides their paid job (e.g., family, other organizing), so even weekly check-ins were difficult to schedule. Logistical challenges may seem mundane, but they are also symptomatic of a culture of busyness that can affect the viability of collaborative projects. The lack of time affects group dynamics as it stands in the way of communication, of relationship building, of having sufficient time to let ideas simmer until something novel emerges, which is the basis for innovation. Furthermore, in our work with community partners we move at the speed of trust, which again requires time and patience.

Scheduling conflicts can also be symptomatic of the larger challenge of obtaining buy-in from our respective employers to do a collaborative project that seems to be outside of our immediate job descriptions. Note too that our group is made up of relatively junior people in our respective institutions, that is, teachers, graduate students, part-time employees, and early career researchers, which have relatively less autonomy to set their own agendas. The school teacher in our group expressed concerns about doing something in his classroom that did not fit the traditional educational curriculum. Not only was the format unusual for a classroom – social science research is not part of the grade 8 social studies education – but the focus on environmental justice could have been problematic in a state with a record of whitewashing its educational curriculum. For context, in 2010, Arizona passed House Bill 2281 to specifically prevent the teaching of Mexican American history, and again in 2021, House Bills 2906 and 2898 were passed to prevent educators from teaching about race. These bills are seldom effective in the way that legislators intend them, but they do have a chilling effect because schools can lose funding or be fined for defying them. The researchers too had concerns about engaging in a participatory action research project. Within academia, participatory action research is considered to be a risky undertaking for early career researchers because it progresses at a slow pace and findings are context-specific, which make them difficult to turn into high-impact publications. As well, participatory action research projects tend to have higher uncertainty over outcomes because, if the collaboration is genuine, these are co-created with community partners, which is not a straightforward process.

Benefits and enablers

One of the reasons why our group worked well together is that we were able to strike a balance between having a shared vision and carving out our own space. As a group we were committed to certain principles for this project. Things like centering student voices, valuing the time with the community, avoiding white saviorism, or embracing uncertainty, were principles that guided how we interacted with each other and with the students. The principles tend to align with the practices of the progressive social movements that we are each part of, thus providing a common baseline.

On the basis of these common principles, we formed a horizontal organization with shared leadership roles. For example, each of us led and designed activities for the classroom for each portion of the program according to our abilities and interests. The activities had to fit in the overall scheme of the course, but there was a lot of freedom to design each portion. There were a lot of complementary talents in the group, which allowed us to create synergies in our work. In addition, as a group we were very good at reading and adapting to the situation. Sometimes we needed course correction in our logistics, for example, delaying an activity; other times it was about the content, for example, we initially wanted to interview students as part of the photovoice method, but it soon became apparent that students felt awkward in interviews, so we decided to rely on the students' written responses only. The will to experiment and the will to change course were essential to working successfully.

A final enabler was the experience that Carrillo and Franco, who is a former school teacher, brought in terms of working with youth. Because the two of them were present in every class, they provided continuity to the project and helped the students understand how all of the pieces fit together. More importantly, they acted as a bridge between researchers, who were not used to working with youth, and the students, who were not used to dealing with researchers. This bridging function is critical to enabling collaborations because it helps to build trust between groups that have different positionalities. People who act as bridges can vouch for parties who do not know each other well and are essential for translating, interpreting, and scoping.

Recommendations and advice

Reflecting on our experience for the past two years, the main advice that stands out is that for partnerships to work, the group has to have a sense of purpose and stay adaptable. In our case, the sense of purpose was given by our connections to social movements so, while we had differences of opinion, everyone shared the objective of lifting up the students. This gave us a common lens from which to judge our actions and make decisions.

The second thing that was important for our group was that we were able to adapt to the changing circumstances, from troubleshooting technological mishaps, to larger conceptual choices, such as changing or adapting an activity. Truthfully working with youth during the height of the coronavirus pandemic meant stepping into difficult and uncertain situations. However, we understood that it was important to meet students where they were and use our work to validate and amplify their perspectives. We often thought of our work as steering rather than controlling and, we believe, the youth appreciate this aspect of our approach.

Next steps for this work

Our greenspace project continues to evolve. We currently recognize three main areas of activity: First, there are the academic outputs based on the analysis of the data collected during the previous two years. An analytical lens is important to understand the richness of the data and to provide insights about how youth think of greenspace and the future of their community. Second, there have been two media stories about our approach. We have sought to challenge the dominant perceptions about this part of the city, and so we worked with specific journalists who are known to challenge the dominant negative discourse about Central City. The first one was entitled ' "You're already experts": South Phoenix students empowered to reimagine their green spaces,' and it came out in the Arizona Republic in May 2021, just as the school year was ending, so the students and their families had a chance to see themselves and their work in the Phoenix local newspaper. The second one was a video by NowThisNews featuring Carrillo on the broader theme of environmental injustice. The third, and perhaps most important outcome of our project is that the '*barrio* innovation' model has inspired us to found a community organization, AZ(Land) (https://azlnd.org) that uses the '*barrio* innovation' approach to tackle issues around environmental and social justice in the community at large. The organization is the vision of Carrillo and Franco, and it will host its first public event in December 2021 at the Nina Mason Pulliam Rio Salado Audubon Center near the school, where we are inviting the community to spend the afternoon engaging in conversations about the past, present, and the future of South of Phoenix, through a series of activities and cultural performances. The goal of this event is to establish our presence in the community and to take the pulse of current concerns among the residents of the area before launching our next research endeavor.

To conclude, during the past three years, our group has experimented with different participatory and creative activities to co-produce positive futures with youth from Academia del Pueblo. Our work, which we choose to call '*barrio* innovation,' has taught us to do research with, rather than in, community. Our approach understands time as dynamic, community as abundant, and rootedness as essential in opening up the solution space toward rectifying historical wrongs and inspiring us to find pathways toward environmental and social justice.

Acknowledgments

This research is based upon the work supported by the National Science Foundation under grant number DEB-1832016, Central Arizona-Phoenix

Long-Term Ecological Research Program (CAP LTER), and SRN-1444755, Urban Resilience to Extreme Events Sustainability Research Network (UREx SRN). Team members would like to thank the students, staff, and families from Academia del Pueblo, and acknowledge the generosity of Sam Gomez and Selina Martinez from The Sagrado Galleria, and Teo Argueta, formerly with Chispa Arizona.

References

Birch, E. L., & Wachter, S. M. (2008). *Growing greener cities*. University of Pennsylvania Press, Philadelphia, PA.

Bolin, B., Grineski, S., & Collins, T. (2005). The geography of despair: Environmental racism and the making of South Phoenix, Arizona, USA. *Human Ecology Review*, 156–168.

Bolin, B., Matranga, E., Hackett, E. J., Sadalla, E. K., Pijawka, K. D., Brewer, D., & Sicotte, D. (2000). Environmental equity in a sunbelt city: The spatial distribution of toxic hazards in Phoenix, Arizona. *Global Environmental Change Part B: Environmental Hazards*, 2(1), 11–24.

Boucher, J. L., Levenda, A. M., Carpenter, C., Morales-Guerrero, J., & Karwat, D. M. (2021). Environmental justice in Phoenix, Arizona: A neighbourhood deficit and asset score. *Local Environment*, 26(6), 692–718. https://doi.org/10.1080/135498 39.2021.1916899

Bullard, R. D. (Eds.). (1994). *Unequal protection: Environmental justice and communities of color*. Sierra Club Books, San Francisco CA.

Bullard, R. D. (2000). *Dumping in Dixie: Race, class, and environmental quality*. New York, NY: Routledge, Taylor & Francis.

Connors, J. P., Galletti, C. S., & Chow, W. T. (2013). Landscape configuration and urban heat island effects: Assessing the relationship between landscape characteristics and land surface temperature in Phoenix, Arizona. *Landscape Ecology*, 28(2), 271–283. https://doi.org/10.1007/s10980-012-9833-1

Cornwall, A., & Jewkes, R. (1995). What is participatory research? *Social Science & Medicine*, 41(12), 1667–1676.

Fraser, N. (2000). Rethinking recognition. *New Left Review*, 3, 107.

Freire, P. (1996). *Pedagogy of the oppressed* (revised ed.). New York: Continuum.

Garfin, G., Jardine, A., Merideth, R., Black, M., & LeRoy, S. (Eds.). (2013). *Assessment of climate change in the southwest United States: A report prepared for the National Climate Assessment*. Washington DC, Island Press/Center for Resource Economics.

Gómez-Baggethun, E., Gren, Å., Barton, D. N., Langemeyer, J., McPhearson, T., O'farrell, P., . . . & Kremer, P. (2013). Urban ecosystem services. In *Urbanization, biodiversity and ecosystem services: Challenges and opportunities* (pp. 175–251). Dordrecht, The Netherlands: Springer.

Hart, J. (2013). *The art of the storyboard: A filmmaker's introduction*. New York, NY Taylor & Francis.

Heynen, N., Perkins, H. A., & Roy, P. (2006). The political ecology of uneven urban green space: The impact of political economy on race and ethnicity in producing environmental inequality in Milwaukee. *Urban Affairs Review, 42*(1), 3–25. https://doi.org/10.1177/1078087406290729

Hough, M. (2004). *Cities and natural process: A basis for sustainability.* London: Routledge.

IPCC. (2021). *Special report: Climate change and land.* Retrieved from www.ipcc.ch/srccl/

Maricopa County Public Health. (2020). *Heat-associated deaths in Maricopa County, AZ: Final report for 2020.* Retrieved from www.maricopa.gov/ArchiveCenter/ViewFile/Item/5240

Mathie, A., & Cunningham, G. (2003). From clients to citizens: Asset-based community development as a strategy for community-driven development. *Development in Practice, 13*(5), 474–486. https://doi.org/10.1080/0961452032000125857

McHarg, I. L. (1969). *Design with nature.* New York: American Museum of Natural History.

McPhearson, T., Hamstead, Z. A., & Kremer, P. (2014). Urban ecosystem services for resilience planning and management in New York City. *Ambio, 43*(4), 502–515. https://doi.org/10.1007/s13280-014-0509-8

Nelson, J. R., Grubesic, T. H., Miller, J. A., & Chamberlain, A. W. (2021). The equity of tree distribution in the most ruthlessly hot city in the United States: Phoenix, Arizona. *Urban Forestry & Urban Greening, 59*, 127016. https://doi.org/10.1016/j.ufug.2021.127016

Pickett, S. T., Cadenasso, M. L., Childers, D. L., McDonnell, M. J., & Zhou, W. (2016). Evolution and future of urban ecological science: Ecology in, of, and for the city. *Ecosystem Health and Sustainability, 2*(7), e01229. https://doi.org/10.1002/ehs2.1229

Pope, C. A., Coleman, N., Pond, Z. A., & Burnett, R. T. (2016). Fine particulate air pollution and human mortality: 25+ years of cohort studies. *Environmental Research, 183*, 18924. https://doi.org/10.1016/j.envres.2019.108924

Rubin, V. (2008). The roots of the urban greening movement. In E. L. Birch & S. M. Wachter (Eds.), *Growing greener cities* (pp. 187–206). Philadelphia, PA: University of Pennsylvania Press.

Schlosberg, D. (2007). *Defining environmental justice: Theories, movements, and nature.* Oxford: Oxford University Press.

Schlosberg, D., & Collins, L. B. (2014). From environmental to climate justice: Climate change and the discourse of environmental justice. *Wiley Interdisciplinary Reviews: Climate Change, 5*(3), 359–374. https://doi.org/10.1002/wcc.275

Stackelberg, P. V. (2011). *Creating digital narratives: The structure and design of stories told across multiple media* (Doctoral dissertation) SUNY Polytechnic Institute, Utica, NY.

USGCRP. (2017). *Climate science special report: Fourth national climate assessment* (Vol. 1) (D. J. Wuebbles, D. W. Fahey, K. A. Hibbard, D. J. Dokken, B. C. Stewart, & T. K. Maycock, Eds.). Washington, DC, USA: U.S. Global Change Research Program, 470 pp, doi: 10.7930/J0J964J6

York, A., Tuccillo, J., Boone, C., Bolin, B. O. B., Gentile, L., Schoon, B., & Kane, K. (2014). Zoning and land use: A tale of incompatibility and environmental injustice in early Phoenix. *Journal of Urban Affairs, 36*(5), 833–853. https://doi.org/10.1111/juaf.12076

Young, I. M. (1990). *Justice and the politics of difference*. Princeton, NJ: Princeton University Press.

Zhang, Y., Murray, A. T., & Turner Ii, B. L. (2017). Optimizing green space locations to reduce daytime and nighttime urban heat island effects in Phoenix, Arizona. *Landscape and Urban Planning, 165*, 162–171. https://doi.org/10.1016/j.landurbplan.2017.04.009

3 Envisioning future scenarios to manage pluvial flooding in social-ecological-technological systems

Jason Sauer, Olga Barbosa, Elizabeth M. Cook, Nancy Grimm, Cristóbal Lamarca, Javiera Maira, Alejandra Schueftan & David M. Iwaniec

Introduction

Cities should be considered as social (S), ecological (E), and technological (T) systems, and environmental stressors in cities will interact with and derive from, social, ecological, and technological domains (Kim et al., 2021; Markolf et al., 2018). For example, the environmental stressor of flooding in a city may have a financial impact on people from some socio-economic groups more than others (S), damage key urban ecosystems and impact biodiversity (E), and disrupt transportation and electricity transmission systems (T). Responding to stressors in one domain will leave the others vulnerable, either directly or through cascading impacts (Rocha et al., 2018). For example, a disrupted transit system (T) may become a threat to the earnings of lower-income individuals without personal vehicles who have come to rely on it (S), or leave them isolated from parks and recreational spaces (E). In order to manage an environmental stressor, all three SETS domains must be considered in understanding the stressor's origins, its impacts, and strategies and solutions for dealing with the stressor.

Flooding is the costliest and one of the most common environmental stressors in urban areas around the world (Hammond et al., 2015; Jha et al., 2012). Pluvial flooding occurs when the rate of precipitation overwhelms the rate of infiltration and the ability of stormwater management systems to remove water from the system. Pluvial flooding is underrepresented in academic literature and in disaster management efforts but is receiving growing attention among academics (Rosenzweig et al., 2018) and city practitioners. Determining the origins of pluvial flooding in cities requires a SETS-based assessment, as the origins are typically a combination of increasing impermeable surfaces (T), design and planning of

DOI: 10.4324/9781003208723-3

stormwater management infrastructure for changing environmental and anthropogenic variables (ST), and obstruction or destruction of natural waterways (E) – and all of these occur according to legacies of marginalization and mistreatment of certain demographic groups (S) (Chang et al., 2021). Solutions to pluvial flooding must then also occur in all three SETS domains. They may require assessment of current and future flood exposure (SET), address histories of inequitable risk and solution distribution among neglected sociodemographic groups (S), incorporate multiple knowledge systems and perspectives (SET), and require the utilization of some combination of green stormwater infrastructure (E), traditional gray stormwater infrastructure (T), and community intervention (S).

Cities may struggle to consider SETS domains in conceptualizations of environmental stressors and solutions due to apparent complexity. Even when cities recognize the SETS domains of stressors and solutions, they may be limited by experience, expertise, and resources to effectively engage all three domains – moreover SETS interactions and tradeoffs. In this chapter we provide the details of an international collaboration among researchers and practitioners, as part of the work of the Urban Resilience to Extremes Sustainability Research Network (UREx SRN), to effect SETS change at city, regional, and national scales. Though we focus specifically on pluvial flooding in Valdivia, Chile, our intention is that this chapter will serve as a reproducible and modifiable blueprint for researchers and practitioners, across the globe, to integrate SETS, when contending with any environmental stressor.

Description of the case study area

Valdivia, Chile (area: 93.94 km^2), is a city of approximately 150,000 people in the southern half of Chile, 850 km south of the capital Santiago, in the Región de los Ríos (Figure 3.1). Valdivia is the capital and the most populous city in its region and is growing in population due to higher birth rates and intra-national and international migration.

Citizens and city managers of Valdivia must contend with a high risk of fluvial and pluvial flooding. Valdivia's flood risk is in part due to geophysical factors, including high annual precipitation (1780 mm), a long wet season, and the city's location 12 km inland from the Pacific Ocean at the confluence of three major rivers. Due to high precipitation and mild temperatures, the local ecosystem is classified as a temperate rainforest (Amigo & Ramirez, 1998; Hajek & Di Castri, 1975). Temperatures rarely fall below freezing during the winter, which is also Valdivia's rainy season. The majority of precipitation falls as rain and frequently leads to pluvial flooding in many locations throughout the city.

38 Jason Sauer et al.

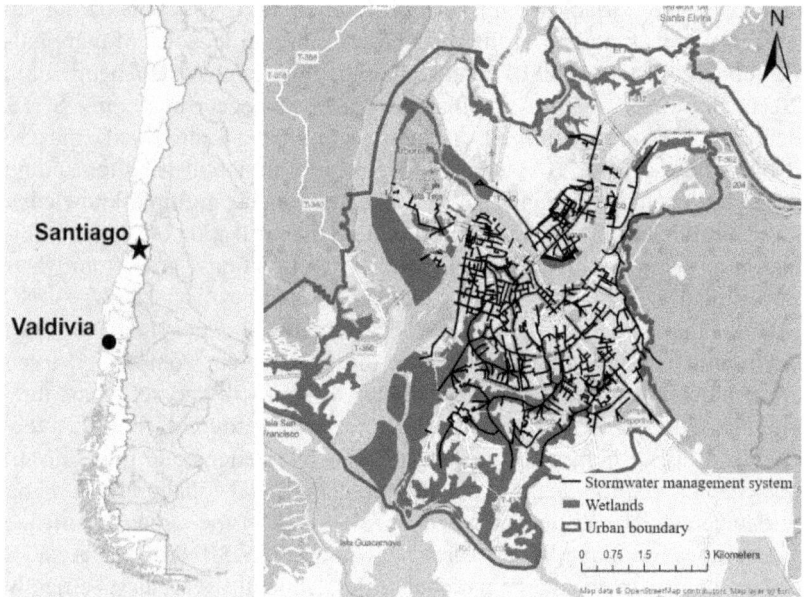

Figure 3.1 Left: location of the study site, Valdivia, Chile (39.8336 S, 73.2154 W). Right: Valdivia's land cover and drainage system in 2012.

Researchers and practitioners in Valdivia

There were several key actors and actor networks in Valdivia concerned with flooding and urban development at the formal start of the collaboration, in 2015, among practitioners in Valdivia and UREx SRN researchers from Chile and the United States. Practitioners involved in collaborations with the Universidad Austral de Chile (UACh), and later with the UREx SRN, included members of the Chilean Forestry Institute (INFOR), a technological research institute of Chile, which operates under the Ministry of Agriculture. INFOR is broadly responsible for generating information on forest resources to be incorporated into territory planning and management instruments. It operates at local and regional scales and has developed a coordinated work model between public institutions and local communities to support decision-making that contributes to the responsible use of forest resources, the conservation of ecosystems, and a better quality of life for the communities that cohabitate with the forest. INFOR has a particular interest in studying the development of peri-urban areas where city growth is often in conflict with managing pluvial flooding and the conservation of natural ecosystems.

Another key actor in prior collaborations with the Universidad Austral de Chile, and later with the UREx SRN, was the head of Activa Valdivia, which is the technical office of the Consorcio Valdivia Sustentable. The Consorcio Valdivia Sustentable is a private organization that seeks to promote the sustainable development of the city through the creation of collaborations between public, private, social, and academic entities. The consortium has been operating since 2012, and its main function is to generate dialogues between local actors in Valdivia, such as the Universidad Austral de Chile; non-profits, such as Visión Valdivia; local businesses, such as Arauco, Valdicor, and Naguilán; and city, regional, and federal agencies, such as the Municipality of Valdivia, the Chilean Ministry of Public Works (MOP), the Chilean Ministry of Transport and Telecommunications, the Chilean Ministry of Housing and Urbanism (MINVU), and the Community Union of the Neighborhood Council, among others. Activa Valdivia, more specifically, provides architectural and urban design solutions to public entities, which in turn finance the implementation of these design solutions. Through Activa Valdivia's model, the cost and management time of urban projects may be reduced, and innovative urban designs, such as green infrastructure, are adopted more quickly.

Stormwater management and wetland conservation

Valdivia's stormwater management system is composed primarily of gray infrastructure components (i.e., concrete pipes and canals) and wetlands (Figure 3.1). Based on a 2012 map of Valdivia's stormwater management system, 204.53 km (83.2%) of the system length is gray infrastructure while 41.19 km (16.8%) is wetland land cover. The origin of most of this wetland cover is a 1960 earthquake of magnitude 9.5, which, in addition to causing up to 20 m of uplift in some areas (Barrientos & Ward, 1990), caused subsidence and rifting in others. Many of these latter areas are now the sites of Valdivia's wetlands, as their bases are now located below the water table and are either seasonally or permanently inundated.

Since the 1960 earthquake, the city has deliberately incorporated wetlands into its stormwater management system improvement plans (CMOP, 2012) as green stormwater infrastructure. In addition, there have been notable local movements to conserve wetland extent for the ecosystem services wetlands provide, such as habitat for biodiversity (Silva et al., 2016), as well as for reasons of environmental justice (Correa et al., 2018). In spite of efforts to conserve and use Valdivia's wetlands as green stormwater infrastructure and as culturally significant features, wetland cover in Valdivia has decreased around 6% since 1960, according to internal UREx SRN analysis. Causes of wetland loss include incidental sedimentation from urban overland flow; illegal, large-scale trash dumping; illegal infilling; and legal land-use conversion, such as the construction of housing, commercial buildings, and university landscaping.

As a green stormwater infrastructure element, wetlands may manage pluvial flooding via several mechanisms. Wetlands may store water, promote infiltration, reduce peak flow depths, and alter peak flow timing (Elmqvist et al., 2016; Kadykalo & Findlay, 2016; Li et al., 2020). They may also remove water from the stormwater management system through evapotranspiration (Bois et al., 2017). The flow of stormwater through Valdivia's stormwater management system may involve passage through gray infrastructure components, wetlands, or both, depending on the point of entrance – the route water takes through Valdivia's stormwater management system can be quite complex. Depending on the route, the antecedent moisture conditions, and the geophysical aspects of the wetlands along a route, they may perform one or all pluvial flood management functions. The ability of the stormwater management system in Valdivia to handle precipitation, and thus manage pluvial flooding, depends on the coupled performances of its gray infrastructure components and its wetland green stormwater infrastructure, and we would expect to see changes in either element affecting the performance of the other.

Rationale for doing this work

The UREx SRN's researchers from the U.S. and Chile sought to collaborate with practitioners in Valdivia for several reasons. First, the UREx SRN's mission was, in part, to conduct multinational research on urban resilience to extreme weather events in U.S. and Latin American cities, for the purpose of including diverse perspectives on vulnerability and resilience. Second, researchers Olga Barbosa, Javiera Maira, and Elizabeth Cook, co-authors of this chapter, had established research efforts on urban sustainability at the Universidad Austral de Chile in Valdivia and were therefore invited to participate in the network. Third, and critically, the researchers in Valdivia had existing contacts and histories of collaboration with private and government practitioners who were concerned with flooding in the city. Even before the UREx SRN project, the researchers and practitioners had a joint interest in collaborating and seeking innovative solutions to address the urban flooding challenges of Valdivia.

Valdivia was an ideal site for research because it allowed researchers to engage with SETS domains from problem conception all the way through solutions and strategies. As an environmental stressor, pluvial flooding in Valdivia was due to a combination of all three SETS domains, such as regional patterns of urbanization (S); heavy rainfall and wetland loss (E); and the proliferation of impermeable surfaces and the design of the stormwater management system (T). Conceptualizing the solutions for pluvial flooding in Valdivia required the involvement of perspectives and expertise in each of the SETS domains.

Furthermore, while much has been written about the general abilities of wetlands to reduce flood risk in cities, at the start of this collaborative work in Valdivia, there had been no study on how the loss of inland wetlands in an urban stormwater management system might affect pluvial flood risk. Chan et al. (2018) have since been proponents of the so-called Sponge City, which constructs inland wetlands to replace less permeable or impermeable land cover to enhance infiltration during rainfall events. However, like Valdivia, many cities across the globe are losing their inland wetlands to development, and there remain no studies on how inland urban wetland loss alters their pluvial flood risk. More research was needed on how inland wetland hydrological dynamics, such as seasonal and annual changes to wetland stage, soil moisture, and evapotranspiration, alter pluvial flood risk in a stormwater management system.

Summarily, Valdivia was a compelling site for research for both practical and academic reasons. Practically, it seemed plausible to accomplish our goal of addressing the stressor of pluvial flooding because of an established relationship between researchers and practitioners in Valdivia. Academically, Valdivia was a novel site for studying the mechanisms behind and impacts of land cover change on pluvial flooding in an urban setting, using SETS analysis.

Details of what was done

The collaborative process between researchers and practitioners was developed by both URBx SRN researchers and practitioner affiliates from Valdivia, in order to ensure appropriate stakeholder involvement in the first workshop. Through surveys and interviews conducted in Valdivia by the URBx SRN team, we were able to create a list of priority topics for discussion and a list of desired stakeholder participants.

This project can be divided into four primary tasks. The first was a workshop held in Valdivia in 2017; next came evaluating and building upon the results of that first workshop; the team then focused on maintaining relationships and interest in the collaboration between 2017 and 2020; and finally, a second workshop was held in 2020.

Scenarios workshop 1

In May 2017, the UREx SRN conducted a workshop in Valdivia, to envision a series of long-term (to the year 2080) future scenarios and desirable future pathways of urban development. The workshop followed protocols developed in the UREx SRN project (Iwaniec et al., 2021) with local and visiting UREx SRN researchers and practitioners as workshop facilitators. This workshop focused on two environmental stressors, drought and pluvial flooding, but for reasons of limited space, this chapter will focus only on pluvial flooding. A second workshop was held in 2019 after analyses were completed from the scenarios produced in the first workshop.

Participants in the workshop in May 2017 represented a diverse array of Valdivia's stakeholders, such as municipal and regional government employees, university professors, students, and members of community action groups. Many of these stakeholders had been working with UREx members at UACh since 2014. Participants of this first workshop were presented with SETS information on pluvial flood exposure and sensitivity in Valdivia, both for the present and for the year 2080. UREx SRN researchers developed visualizations of present-day pluvial flood exposure; pluvial flood sensitivity using 19 different social, ecological, and technological variables of flood vulnerability, similar to those in Table 3.1 (and similar to work done in Chang et al., 2021); and a combined vulnerability index where the exposure (E) and sensitivity (ST) layers were overlaid (Figure 3.2). Participants were also presented with downscaled climate model projections of heat and precipitation for Valdivia, produced by UREx SRN researchers, which indicated that the annual incidence of the most intense storms would increase by the year 2080, thereby potentially increasing the risk of major pluvial flooding (Kunkel, 2017).

Table 3.1 List of SETS variables used in sensitivity analysis in Valdivia, Chile.

SETS metric	SETS dimension
Past pluvial flood exposure	E
Population, over 65 years of age	S
Population, between 0 and 5 years of age	S
Population, indigenous	S
Population, immigrant	S
Home, type: mobile	T
Home, walls: precarious materials	T
Home, floors: dirt floors	T
Home, material quality: unrecoverable	T
Water source: water truck	T
Water source: rivers, lakes, estuaries	T

Envisioning future scenarios to manage pluvial flooding 43

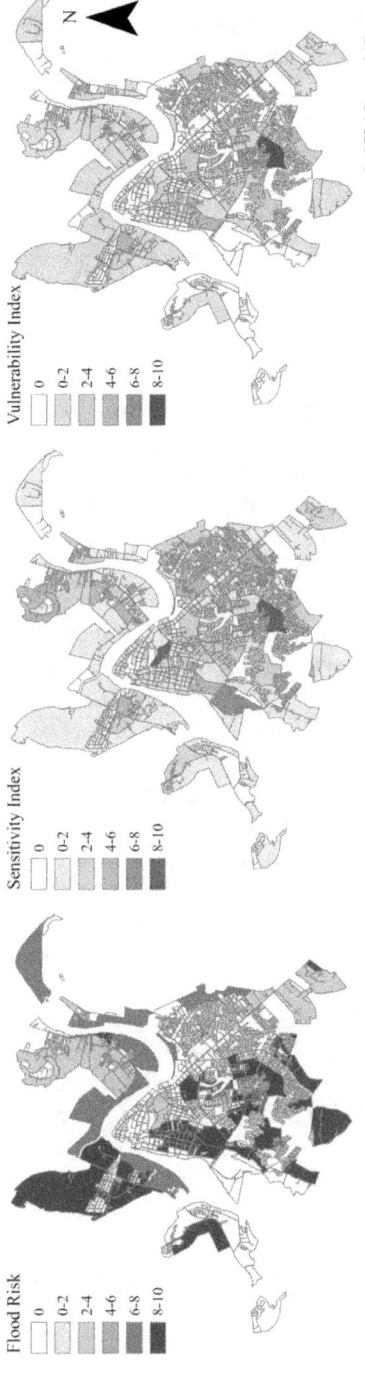

Figure 3.2 Left: Visualization of recorded pluvial flooding (known as flood exposure or flood risk) in Valdivia, Chile, in 2016. Middle: Visualization of the degree of impact (sensitivity) that pluvial flooding would be likely to have, using ten metrics of social and technological vulnerability characteristics, collected from the 2017 census. Right: Visualization of vulnerability to flooding, created by multiplying the Flood Risk index by the Sensitivity index, and normalizing between 0 and 10. In all three maps, 0 represents the lowest risk of experiencing damage from pluvial flooding and 10 represents the highest risk.

After being presented with information on pluvial flooding, participants collaborated to develop a suite of visions and strategies to undertake to achieve five unique, desirable and plausible scenarios for a future Valdivia: an Inclusive City, a Friendly City, an Eco-Wetland City, and a Flood- and Drought-Resilient City. These scenario themes emerged from the concerns of the citizens of Valdivia and analysis of Valdivia's governance documents, including work from the Inter-American Development Bank (IDB, 2015). From these themes, the visioning and scenario development process in the workshop followed methods described by Iwaniec et al. (2021), using co-production techniques described by Cook et al. (2021). The end results were participant visions of a future Valdivia that would be more resilient to pluvial flooding and heat waves.

For the Inclusive City scenario, participants emphasized education based on sustainability; the implementation of neighborhood 'kits' as spaces for civil participation and sources of urban services; an environmental social justice approach; and a broader focus on people, a safe city, and equitability. Participants in this scenario recognized that inclusivity must be complemented with resilience to floods and drought scenarios due to the differential impacts they may have on the socio-economic groups in Valdivia.

For the Friendly City scenario, participants emphasized the concepts of citizen participation, territorial equity, prevalence of meeting spaces, guaranteeing access to critical infrastructure and transport services, reordering the image of the city through its facades, and involving the natural environment, such as Valdivia's natural wetlands and forests, as part of urban planning.

For the Flood and Drought Resilient City scenario, this group highlighted the need for greater densification within the city, integrated management of the city watershed with systems-oriented vision, the need to stimulate innovation to create solutions to environmental stressors, education based on the city's fluvial (river-adjacent) identity, and the need for transitional spaces.

For the Eco-Wetland City scenario, participants emphasized the prioritization of the development of a better urban land governance model, greater understanding of the laws that regulate wetland management, greater integration and restoration of historic areas that historically connected the wetlands, the demonstration of the values that proximity to wetlands provide, and more citizen participation in decisions surrounding wetland management.

Evaluation of results: workshop 1

Between workshops, the positive visioning process (Iwaniec et al., 2021) recommends the assessment of workshop outputs for their likelihoods and abilities to bring about the desired visions of the workshop participants. These assessments may include the qualitative analysis of the workshop outcomes and process, quantitative modeling of the effects the scenarios may have on the stressors being evaluated, design-based renderings of these envisioned cities, and data visualization (Iwaniec et al., 2021). These assessments are intended to be used during the second workshop in order to allow participants to reflect on the workshop 1 process, to evaluate whether their scenario goals would be met, and to weigh the tradeoffs of pursuing different visions of the city.

One assessment that UREx SRN researchers pursued was the preparation of future land cover maps of Valdivia. All workshop 1 scenarios involved considerations of the environment, and wetlands in particular, and estimates of future land cover provided a useful assessment to prepare for workshop 2. The UREx SRN modeling team used scenario objectives and historical land cover data on Valdivia from 1983 to 2010 in a cellular automata-based model (Soares-Filho et al., 2001, 2002) of land use/land cover (LULC) change to produce estimates of LULC in Valdivia in 2080 (Sauer et al., in review). From these model outputs, participants in workshop 2 would be able to assess how the layout of the city would be changed by their vision, and how access to wetland, forest, and park spaces might be affected.

UREx SRN researchers also produced renderings of different areas of Valdivia in 2080 according to each scenario. These renderings portrayed changes in the social, ecological, and technological fabric of the city based on the objectives outlined in each vision. Renderings were of locations in the city that were readily recognizable by the average Valdivian citizen, such as a popular walkway along the Calle-Calle River or a street normally dominated by vehicle traffic. These illustrations included people, plants, animals, and built infrastructure, to make participants think in a less technical way about how they were affecting the SETs domains of the city.

Regular meetings of collaborators and workshop participants: Mesas de Trabajo

In order to maintain working relationships and momentum with workshop 1 participants, particularly with our municipal practitioners, regular meetings were scheduled at biannual intervals. Four *Mesas de Trabajo* ('work tables') were held between workshop 1 in 2017 and workshop 2 in 2020. These meetings typically lasted for a morning or afternoon session, and were intended to include as many workshop 1 participants as responded to invitation. Mesas de Trabajo were designed as spaces for UREx SRN researchers to give updates on progress toward workshop 2, and for participants to review the goals set forth for workshop 2 and voice any concerns about progress or new developments in the city that should be considered for workshop 2. These *Mesas de Trabajo* also served as spaces where researchers and practitioners could engage about topics beyond the scope of the workshops, such as about recent flood events or development expansions in ecologically sensitive areas. We found that these regular meetings helped to reaffirm trust between participants, and in some cases they served as starting points for new collaborations.

Scenarios workshop 2

The second UREx SRN scenarios workshop was planned to be held in October 2019. The same participants in the 2017 workshop were invited to attend, as well as some other figures who either had since replaced original participants in their organizations or had emerged as relevant parties. However, due to nationwide civil unrest that began the weekend before the workshop was scheduled, we scheduled several in-group meetings so that the Chile-based UREx SRN affiliates could hold the workshop at a later time when it became possible. In March of 2020, UREx SRN members in Valdivia scheduled a second scenarios workshop and project update.

This second workshop was structured in four stages, complemented with reception, coffees, introduction, and a closing discussion. These four stages were (1) an overview that included a presentation and explanation of the UREx SRN project, a review of the concepts of resilience and sustainability, and a review of the work carried out in workshop 1; (2) a 'gallery walk,' where assistants presented posters on the scenarios from workshop 1, including LULC analysis and renderings and, with the help of a team facilitator, provided assessments of the benefits and drawbacks of each one; (3) a breakout into working groups according to scenario, where participants were asked to voice positive and negative characteristics they viewed in their scenario and where participants were also asked to identify the steps and actors to engage in order to achieve implementation of the positive characteristics; and (4) a plenary session where each working group presented to the full audience of attendees the positive characteristics they identified as well as the steps and actors they would engage to achieve them, in order to solicit response and commentary from participants not involved in the specific scenario working group (Mannetti et al., 2021).

The Valdivia team drew valuable elements from each scenario as discussed in the workshop, and one of the general conclusions was the need to work toward a combined scenario integrating the main attributes highlighted in the breakout groups. This task is still pending; however, there is consensus on the structural guidelines, such as the need to densify and control urban sprawl, and to incorporate 'green areas' for flood regulation, temperature regulation, and as spaces for social integration. Furthermore, the promotion of social capital and good governance was present in the narratives produced by workshop participants.

Outcomes

The primary goal of this collaboration was to use SETS theory to characterize an environmental stressor, to co-produce strategies to manage this stressor that would cover each SETS domain, and to turn those strategies into solutions that crossed all domains. The work in this collaboration, as it has been described so far, was successful in achieving the first two goals, but is still being realized toward achieving the third goal. We highlight here the ongoing work of our UREx SRN affiliates, researchers, and extended community.

Activa Valdivia

For Activa Valdivia, this collaboration has allowed for the articulation of a clear vision for the urban future of Valdivia, based on climate projections and the visions developed in the workshops. As part of the adaptation strategies toward Valdivia's resilience to environmental stressors like heat waves and pluvial flooding, Activa Valdivia is pursuing an urban development paradigm of nature-based solutions such as green, blue, and hybrid infrastructures. These forms of infrastructure provide critical ecosystem services to Valdivia in all three social, ecological, and technological domains. As a complement to this pursuit, by the recommendation of our UREx SRN affiliate in Activa Valdivia, the Sustainable Valdivia Consortium has promoted an orientation to SETS considerations to the members and missions of its board of directors.

Some example projects in Valdivia under development that have been developed with SETS considerations are the Las Ánimas Fluvial Park, Matta Fluvial Station, Yañez Zabala Wetland Park, Fluvial Master Plan, and Sponge plaza barrios bajos, among others (Figure 3.3). In addition, the first pilot sponge plaza, designed using SETS theory, has already been implemented in the city and has withstood intense rains and reduced runoff in the area.

Among our outcomes, the work done by Activa Valdivia as a result of its involvement was for us one of the most unexpected successes of the work. Although we had of course hoped to instill SETS thinking in the work of our UREx SRN researchers and UREx SRN affiliates, Activa Valdivia has gone beyond and is now flying the SETS banner in all of its work.

Figure 3.3 Matta Fluvial Station, being developed by Activa Valdivia, incorporates SETS principles.

Infor

Infor is collaborating on a project that develops technologies focused on resilience and adaptability to climate change, along with principles of sustainability. Pilot projects of wastewater-purifying wetlands are being developed as a solution in both rural and peri-urban areas.

National wetland protection law

In January 2020, Chile passed a law modifying various existing statutes on environmental protection in order to conserve the nation's urban wetlands. This new law is regarded as one of the widest-reaching and strictest environmental protection laws the country has ever passed. Passing this law also required the convening of several panels of scientists working in Chilean wetlands in order to construct and confirm an inventory of urban wetlands and to determine the potential threats that urban areas pose to the integrity of wetlands. Due to their previous collaborations with wetland scientists and practitioners in Valdivia, done as part of the work described in this chapter, a UREx SRN researcher was invited to serve on this panel. By applying SETS theory to the stressor of urban populations on wetlands, the panel was able to identify threats to wetland integrity from each SETS domain, such as illegal dumping (S), changes in the timing and amount of annual rainfall due to climate change (E), and high flows due to urban stormwater infrastructure and impervious surfaces (T). Hopefully, introducing SETS considerations into the process will allow for a more complete set of strategies to manage stressors on urban wetlands.

Research directions

In considering the stressor of pluvial flooding in Valdivia, and the links in Valdivia among pluvial flooding, its stormwater management system, and its wetland cover, we have come to realize that there is a gap in the academic literature on the effects of inland urban wetland loss on pluvial flooding in cities. Furthermore, we realized that there is a notable lack of existing studies on urban wetland hydrological dynamics, such as changing soil moisture conditions, changing surface water storage, evapotranspiration, and the ability of wetlands to mitigate floods. As cities across the globe are expanding their footprints, often into areas with wetland cover, they would benefit from understanding how their pluvial flood risk will change with wetland loss, or, in the case that they conserve their wetlands, with changing hydrological conditions in wetlands. Researchers with the UREx SRN are currently producing research on these topics using data collected from Valdivian wetlands as part of this collaboration.

Reflections

Barriers and obstacles

We will not be the first collaboration between academics and practitioners to highlight our difficulties in managing the difference in expected time frames of work between these groups, but they are nonetheless worth highlighting. SETS considerations are complex and may take a considerable amount of time for academic researchers to assess and translate to actionable outputs. As such, our researchers had three years between workshop 1 and workshop 2 to turn the various outcomes of workshop 1 into decision support data for workshop 2, and had mixed success in doing so, to some disappointment by our practitioner partners.

In addition to working cross-sectorally, this collaboration also involved working across international borders. We faced challenges of linking cultures and international trends on the transformative perspectives that cities require to manage environmental stressors. We also had to manage local contingencies and the difficulty of pursuing visions of the future outside of local reality. Doing so required a transformative look on the part of Chilean public services that went beyond current laws and existing infrastructure. At many times, it was difficult to find solutions to overcome these obstacles and some failures to do so had to be accepted.

Another obstacle encountered in the process of the workshops was that the representatives of the public services that participated in workshop 1 were not all available for workshop 2, having left their positions in the period between workshops. Although in many cases new representatives from the same public service organizations attended, we had to rebuild trust and explain anew the structure of the UREx SRN network as well as the objectives and motivations for our cross-sectoral work.

Benefits and enablers

The main benefit was that after years of work by the UREx SRN researchers and practitioners in Valdivia, it was possible to create a shared discourse on what urban resilience is in Valdivia and why it is important. Further, we learned how through some concrete actions, such as the implementation of green infrastructure, cities can pursue their resilience goals. Today, the broader community linked to the UREx SRN understands these concepts, and that understanding has generated an important cultural base to be able to develop transformative designs that accelerate urban adaptation.

Another relevant benefit for our practitioner affiliates, such as Activa Valdivia, was that this work provided credibility, through the concept of scientific, evidence-based resilience, to discussions of urban intervention. Additionally, in general terms, the workshops were successful, since the workshop objectives were met. The workshops hosted a large audience across a span of expertise and experiences, and the expected products were generated, especially in workshop 1. Workshop 2 had some difficulties typical of the Chilean local contingencies, but was successful in its own right, given the circumstances under which it was held.

Finally, the Valdivia team notes that this collaboration helped to raise awareness of the urgency of incorporating urban resilience criteria into planning, in the face of extreme events and climate change. Turning awareness into momentum requires continual work. There remains among the Valdivia team and workshop participants an improved capacity to understand the city as a system, which permeates their work in other initiatives, plans, and programs.

Recommendations and advice

As others consider the development of scenario workshops and other activities in a cross-sectoral, and perhaps even international, effort like ours, we offer a few suggestions to help jump-start and sustain the collaboration.

The UREx SRN began work in Valdivia in the context of already-established relationships, such as those between researchers Barbosa and Cook, and with practitioners, such as Activa Valdivia. This was, indeed, the primary reason that Valdivia was selected for inclusion in the UREx SRN. It takes time and patience to establish working relationships among academics, practitioners, and communities, sometimes referred to as 'working at the speed of trust,' and we strongly recommend building on extant relationships and collaborations.

Furthermore, we recommend to others that they generate their collaboration alliances with experiences that create trust. For example, we recommend that others develop collaboration activities not limited to simply attending workshops but include other instances of shared experience such as urban walks with stories, recreational activities that center on urban resilience, or even link resilience to other more social characteristics of city dwellers.

We also recommend that researchers be realistic about what they are able to accomplish given the time frames in which practitioner collaborators operate. At the very least, researchers should communicate regularly in the instances that there is a long period of turnaround or they will risk losing practitioner interest or support. Research projects are often ambitious, which is good, but expectations of all of those involved in collaborations should be kept in mind.

Collaborations should take into account personnel churn in practitioner and government agencies. Beyond having to make up for the loss of information that comes with churn, trusting relationships must be reestablished. If the churn happens late in the collaboration, time may be insufficient to truly reestablish such relationships; however, regular communication and meetings with collaborator groups can help make up for earlier churn.

Next steps for this work

The Valdivian researcher practice team is using the climate projection data created by the research team, as well as the process and outcome of co-developing the shared visions of the city's future through the achievement of concrete measures. We come away from this work understanding infrastructure as hybrid solutions that must solve for stressors in multiple SETS domains rather than a single one. As we are writing this chapter, co-author Lamarca, who is a member of Activa Valdivia, is proposing several challenges to the urban form of Valdivia that all have their basis in the visions we co-developed in the scenarios workshops (Activa Valdivia, n.d.).

Acknowledgments

This work would not have been possible without the theoretical contributions, practical expertise, workshop design, and workshop execution of fellow UREx SRN researchers Dr. Marta Berbéz-Blázquez (Arizona State University) and Dr. Tischa Muñoz-Erickson (USDA Forest Service).

References

Activa Valdivia. (n.d.). *Plaza Philippi, Valdivia*. Retrieved from https://activavaldivia.cl/portfolio/plaza-philippi-valdivia/

Amigo, J., & Ramírez, C. (1998). A bioclimatic classification of Chile: Woodland communities in the temperate zone. *Plant Ecology, 136*, 9–26. https://doi.org/10.1023/A:100971420917

Barrientos, S. E., & Ward, S. N. (1990). The 1960 Chile earthquake: Inversion for slip distribution from surface deformation. *Geophysical Journal International, 103*(3), 589–598. https://doi.org/10.1111/j.1365-246X.1990.tb05673.x

Bois, P., Childers, D., Corlouer, T., Laurent, J., Massicot, A., Sanchez, C. A., & Wanko, A. (2017). Confirming a plant-mediated "Biological Tide" in an aridland constructed treatment wetland. *Ecosphere, 8*(3), e01756. https://doi.org/10.18352/ijc.85610.1002/ecs2.1756

Chan, F. K. S., Griffiths, J. A., Higgitt, D., Xu, S., Zhu, F., Tang, Y.-T., Xu, Y., Thorneh, C.R. (2018). "Sponge city" in China: A breakthrough of planning and flood risk management in the urban context. *Land Use Policy, 76*, 772–778. https://doi.org/10.1016/j.landusepol.2018.03.005

Chang, H., Pallathadka, A., Sauer, J., Grimm, N. B., Zimmerman, R., Cheng, C., ... Herreros-Cantis, P. (2021). Assessment of urban flood vulnerability using the social-ecological-technological systems framework in six US cities. *Sustainable Cities and Society, 68*. https://doi.org/10.18352/ijc.85610.1016/j.scs.2021.102786

Cook, E. M., Berbés-Blázquez, M., Mannetti, L. M., Grimm, N. B., Iwaniec, D. M., & Muñoz-Erickson, T. A. (2021). Setting the stage for co-production. In Z. A. Hamstead, D. M. Iwaniec, T. McPhearson, & M. Berbés-Blázquez (Eds.), *Resilient urban futures* (1st ed., pp. 99–111). Springer. https://doi.org/10.1007/978-3-030-63131-4

Correa, H., Blanco-Wells, G., Berrena, J., & Tacón, A. (2018). Self-organizing processes in urban green commons: The case of the Angachilla wetland, Valdivia-Chile. *International Journal of the Commons, 12*(1), 573–595. https://doi.org/10.18352/ijc.856

Elmqvist, T., Setälä, H., Handel, S., van der Ploeg, S., Aronson, J., Blignaut, J. N., Gómez-Baggethun, E., Nowak, D.J., Kronenberg, J., Groot, R. (2016). Benefits of restoration of ecosystem services in cities. *Current Opinion in Environmental Sustainability, 14*, 101–108. https://doi.org/10.1016/j.cosust.2015.05.001

Hajek, E., & Di Castri, F. (1975). Bioclimatografía de Chile. In *Dirección de investigación*. Rectoría Académica, Universidad Católica de Chile.

Hammond, M. J., Chen, A. S., Djordjević, S., Butler, D., & Mark, O. (2015). Urban flood impact assessment: A state-of-the-art review. *Urban Water Journal, 12*(1), 14–29. https://doi.org/10.1080/1573062x.2013.857421

Inter-American Development Bank (IDB). (2015). Valdivia sostenible: Plan de acción.

Iwaniec, D. M., Berbés-Blázquez, M., Cook, E. M., Grimm, N. B., Mannetti, L. M., McPhearson, T., & Muñoz-Erickson, T. A. (2021). Positive Futures. In Z. A. Hamstead, D. M. Iwaniec, T. McPhearson, & M. Berbés-Blázquez (Eds.), *Resilient urban futures* (1st ed., pp. 85–97). Springer. https://doi.org/10.1007/978-3-030-63131-4

Jha, A. K., Bloch, R., & Lamond, J. (2012). *Cities and flooding: A guide to integrated urban flood risk management for the 21st century*. World Bank Publications.

Kadykalo, A. N., & Findlay, C. S. (2016). The flow regulation services of wetlands. *Ecosystem Services*, *20*, 91–103. https://doi.org/10.1016/j.ecoser.2016.06.005

Kim, Y., Mannetti, L. M., Iwaniec, D. M., Grimm, N. B., Berbés-Blázquez, & Markolf, S. (2021). Social, ecological, and technological strategies for climate adaptation. In Z. A. Hamstead & D. M. Iwaniec (Eds.). https://doi.org/10.1007/978-3-030-63131-4_3.

Kunkel, K. (2017). Scenarios of climate extremes: Valdivia, Chile. Internal report from NSF Urban Resilience to Extreme Events SRN #1444755.

Li, Y., Li, H. X., Huang, J., & Liu, C. (2020). An approximation method for evaluating flash flooding mitigation of sponge city strategies: A case study of Central Geelong. *Journal of Cleaner Production*, *257*, 120525. https://doi.org/10.1016/j.jclepro.2020.120525

Mannetti, L. M., Berbés-Blázquez, M., Cook, E. M., Iwaniec, D. M., Grimm, N. B., Lloyd, R., McPhearson, T., & Muñoz-Erickson, T. A. (2021). The UREx guide to scenarios. NSF Urban Resilience to Extremes Sustainability Research Network (UREx SRN).

Markolf, S. A., Chester, M. V., Eisenberg, D. A., Iwaniec, D. M., Davidson, D. I., Zimmerman, R., Miller, T. R., Ruddell, B. L., & Chang, H. (2018). Interdependent infrastructure as linked social, ecological, and technological systems (SETs) to address lock-in and enhance resilience. *Earth's Future*, *6*(12), 1638–1659. https://doi.org/10.1029/2018EF000926

Ministerio de Obras Públicas de Chile (CMOP). (2012). *Plan maestro de evacuación y drenaje de aguas lluvias*. Santiago, Chile: Ministerio de Obras Públicas.

Rocha, J. C., Peterson, G., Bodin, Ö., & Levin, S. (2018). Cascading regime shifts within and across scales. *Science*, *362*, 1379–1383. https://doi.org/10.1126/science.aat7850

Rosenzweig, B., McPhillips, L., Chang, H., Cheng, C., Welty, C., Matsler, M., . . . Davidson, C. I. (2018). Pluvial flood risk and opportunities for resilience. *Water*, *5*(1). https://doi.org/10.1002/wat2.1302

Sauer, J., Cook, E. M., Grimm, N. B., Barbosa, O., Mustafa, A., & McPhearson, T. (In review). Impacts of changing wetland cover on pluvial flood risk in Valdivia, Chile. Earth's Future.

Silva, C. P., Sepulveda, R. D., & Barbosa, O. (2016). Nonrandom filtering effect on birds: Species and guilds response to urbanization. *Ecology and Evolution*, *6*(11), 3711–3720. https://doi.org/10.1002/ece3.2144

Soares-Filho, B. S., Assunção, R., & Pantuzzo, A. (2001). Modeling the spatial transition probabilities of landscape dynamics in an Amazonian colonization frontier. *BioScience*, *51*, 1039–1046. https://doi.org/10.1641/0006-3568(2001)051[1059:MTSTPO]2.0.CO2

Soares-Filho, B. S., Pennachin, C. L., & Cerqueira, G. (2002). DINAMICA a stochastic cellular automata model designed to simulate the landscape dynamics in an Amazonian colonization frontier. *Ecological Modeling*, *154*(3), 217–235. https://doi.org/10.1016/S0304-3800(02)00059-5

4 Co-evolution of resilience initiatives toward a resilience collaboration

Tiffany G. Troxler & Jane Gilbert

Introduction

Institutionalizing long-lasting partnerships among academia and local government colleagues is a challenging endeavor. Impossibly dense schedules, constant fire-fighting, and job turnover are among only a few. But the sense of place and people and the prospects for improving the environment and quality of life of fellow residents keep us engaged. The opportunities for learning, getting to know our neighbors, and training students and staff to observe, study, and understand how they can better prepare and adapt to the impacts and mitigate the causes of climate change drives our ambition to continue to do better. In this chapter, we highlight a progression of initiatives rooted in academic-practitioner partnerships that evolved into an amazing program of work that continues to grow and evolve. We describe the co-evolution of a number of resilience initiatives aimed at reducing flooding impacts due to sea level rise and impacts of increasing and extreme heat in South Florida's Greater Miami and the Beaches (GM&B).

Description of the case study area

South Florida's Greater Miami and the Beaches (GM&B) is among the most vulnerable to compounding hazards of both acute shocks (hurricanes, heavy rain, and extreme heat) and chronic stressors (sea level rise, sunny day flooding, saltwater intrusion, and warming) in the United States (Hallegatte et al., 2013). The GM&B regional 2019 population was 2.7 million with 34 municipalities and a large Miami-Dade County unincorporated municipal service area that supports approximately half of its population. Miami-Dade County provides water and sewer services, transit, environmental regulation, public housing, emergency management, property tax assessment, and social services, while local cities may provide their own police, fire, public works, solid waste, and building permitting.

DOI: 10.4324/9781003208723-4

Among those 34 municipalities is the City of Miami, the central and most populous City occupying 35.9 square miles of land area in 2010. In 2019, its population was nearly 468,000 (US Census Bureau, 2010) with a 17% increase since 2010. The demographic makeup comprises approximately 73% Hispanic or Latino, 11% White, non-Hispanic or Latino, 17% Black or African American and about 1% other races. The median household income is $39,050, and 23.4% of the population lives in poverty. About 33% of households do not have a broadband internet subscription and 70% of the population does not have a bachelor's or higher degree education (of persons aged 25 or over).

City of Miami has a mayor-commissioner form of city government. The mayor is the city's executive and is directly elected; the mayor appoints a city manager to act as Miami's chief administrative officer. Each of the five city commissioners represents a unique geographic district within the city. Development within the City is governed by the Miami21 zoning code and the Florida Building Code. Miami21 is a form-based code guide by the tenets of New Urbanism and Smart Growth. The Florida Building Code is based on the International Building Code and includes the highest hurricane-resistant standards in the country. In addition to climate change, the most significant pressures influencing the city's politics are rapid urbanization, high and increasing income disparity, lack of affordable housing, aging or insufficient infrastructure, and public safety.

Rationale for doing this work

As Miami struggles with its climate-related challenges, it is nonetheless a growing global economic hub, world tourist destination, and the gateway to a number of world-class natural treasures including Everglades National Park, Biscayne National Park, and the Dry Tortugas with Port Miami known as 'The Cruise Capital of the World.' Across the GM&B region, the Greater Miami Convention and Visitors Bureau reported 24 million total visitors, total economic impact of $18 billion in 2019, and a record 147,000 jobs in the travel and hospitality sector alone (GMCVB, 2019). At the edge of the Everglades, the economic output of recreational fishing alone was estimated at $1.2 billion annually (Fedler, 2009), with investment in the largest restoration project in the world anticipated to return 4:1 to Florida's economy and nearly 450,000 jobs over 50 years (McCormick et al., 2010).

So how will we manage the increasing pressures of climate-related challenges, protect and improve environmental quality, and maintain and increase community health and economic vitality in an equitable and just way for all residents? How and what can we learn while we are managing

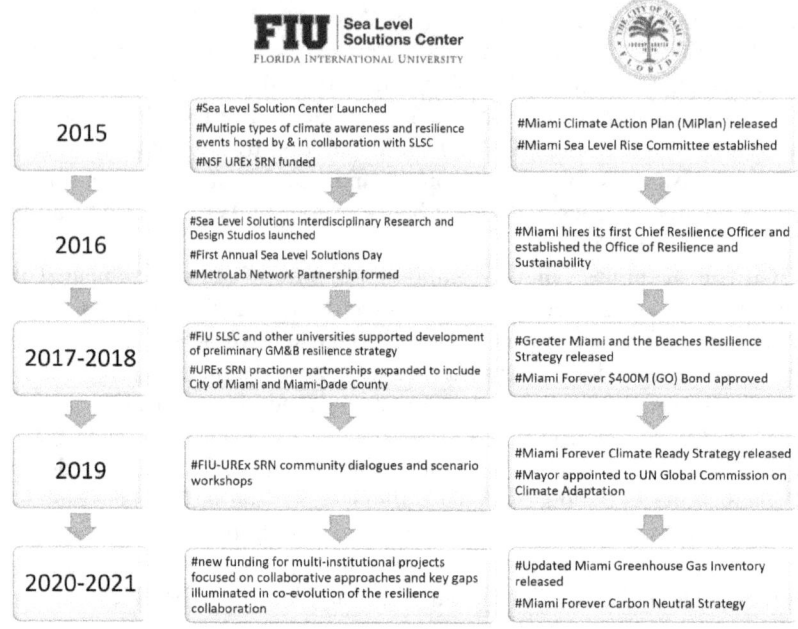

Figure 4.1 Timeline of plans and programs integral to initiating, fostering, and sustaining the partnership of the FIU Sea Level Solutions Center in the Institute of Environment at Florida International University and the City of Miami, Florida.

these challenges to foster broader community-focused outcomes we envision as we work toward building resilience and sustainability in Miami and across the GM&B region? These broad questions motivate our research and serve the common foundation for the academic–practitioner partnerships we work to create. The interplay between policy- and action-oriented outcomes driven by science and knowledge created by our collaborative approach has enabled us to support more informed and effective decision-making by elected leaders and community members. The collaborative partnership and outcomes we achieved were initiated, fostered, and sustained through a series of plans and programs focused on building resilience in the GM&B (Figure 4.1).

How climate change work was elevated at FIU

In July 2015, FIU launched the Sea Level Solutions Center (SLSC) – a hub for interdisciplinary research to support science-based decision-making on climate change mitigation and adaptation. The Center convened and collaborated on a number of community engagement activities to develop a better understanding of the climate-related issues important to our community and what was being done to address them. That Fall, in town were Al Gore's Climate Reality Leadership Corps and FEMA's National Exercise Division, the Miami-Dade County's Sea Level Rise Task Force released its report, and the Southeast Regional Climate Compact released its second edition of the Unified Sea Level Rise Projections for Southeast Florida. The SLSC held its first citizen science flood reporting event in the Shorecrest neighborhood, in partnership with FIU's Department of Journalism in the College of Communications, Architecture, and the Arts (CARTA) and The CLEO Institute, and Xavier Cortada presented his CLIMA exhibit in partnership with the City of Hialeah.

In 2015, we'd also seen the greatest number of high tide events in the past 20 years (Compact, 2019). Miami-Dade's mayor allocated nearly $400K for the Office of Resilience and appointed its first Chief Resilience Officer (CRO). This all following the National Geographic's Treading Water article and the Dutch Water Envoy's damming of Miami as 'The new Atlantis' earlier that year. That Fall, the SLSC was also a co-awardee of the National Science Foundation's Urban Resilience to Extremes Sustainability Research Network (UREx SRN), which helped to catalyze some of the research we were taking on at the Center, and it was a tremendous opportunity to expand our network of faculty collaborating on similar community-engaged research. The UREx SRN Miami city team included faculty in social and ecological sciences and partnered with the City of Miami Beach as the lead practitioner.

FIU SLSC's research in this area expanded through sustained collaboration with CARTA faculty at the Miami Beach Urban Studios in an inaugural semester course to create climate-responsive solutions using a multi-dimensional, integrated social, ecological, and engineering approach – the SLSC interdisciplinary studio. This course focused science-based decision-making on climate change mitigation and adaptation at the project level and began with sustainable and resilient studio projects created for Historic Virginia Key Beach Park. Later projects focused on neighborhoods in Miami Beach and Key Largo, Florida.

How climate change work was elevated at the City of Miami

The importance of addressing climate change in Miami was first elevated by Mayor Manny Diaz, during his second term in 2005–2009. At this time, Mayor Diaz had an increasing leadership role in the US Conference of Mayors and then became the chair and hosted its annual conference in 2008. It was at this time that the mayor wanted to send a strong message that the City was committed to take action on climate and released the City of Miami's first Climate Action Plan, MiPlan. Climate adaptation efforts began under Mayor Regalado in 2015 with the establishment of Sea Level Rise Committee, and in 2016 when City of Miami, City of Miami Beach, and Miami Dade County joined efforts in the creation of a unified Resilience Strategy, hired its first CRO, and established the Office of Resilience and Sustainability. In addition to co-developing a regional resilience Strategy, *Resilient305* (2019), the city began addressing its own adaptation and infrastructure planning with the development and passage of the Miami Forever Bond in 2017 (a $400 million General Obligation bond to support infrastructure investments in stormwater and flood prevention [$192M], affordable housing [$100 million], parks [$78 million], roadways [$23 million], and public safety [$7 million]), and the development of a comprehensive climate adaptation plan, the Miami Forever Climate Ready Strategy in 2019. As a result of these leadership activities, Mayor Suarez was appointed to the UN Global Commission on Climate Adaptation. The city then released an update to the city's greenhouse gas inventory in 2020 and its Miami Forever Carbon Neutral Strategy in April 2021 with goals of a 60% reduction in community-wide GHG emissions by 2035 and carbon neutrality by 2050.

Details of what was done

Engagement and data to increase the understanding of sea level rise impacts

The city's partnership with Florida International University's Sea Level Solutions Center began in 2015 when FIU held its first citizen science documentation of the flood depths in low-lying Shorecrest neighborhood. These data were helpful in documenting the extent of these tides and communicating the increasing inundation risks facing the city. In 2016, the city expanded this effort to include locations throughout the City of Miami and Miami Beach with its first annual Sea Level Solutions Day, a citizen science effort that involved students and residents documenting and witnessing the changes happening in their city as a result of sea level rise and climate change. These efforts provided data to support the need for an updated stormwater master plan and a general obligation bond to begin finance infrastructure upgrades. Since 2016, the city has helped promote, participated in, and often hosted the orientation/training sessions associated with the annual Sea Level Solutions Day event.

Supporting the Resilient305 strategy

Also around 2016, the same time of the formation of the partnership between Miami-Dade County, City of Miami, and City of Miami Beach to jointly apply to become part of the Rockefeller Foundation's 100 Resilient Cities program, MetroLab had invited the same jurisdictions individually to consider applying in partnership with a local university to participate in the MetroLab Network. The MetroLab Network is an international collaborative of over 30 cities and universities focused on civic research and innovation. The decision was made to use the GM&B partnership as the foundation for the MetroLab participation; to include the three largest local academic institutions: Miami Dade College, Florida International University, and the University of Miami; and to focus on three primary areas of mutual interest: pandemic response (Greater Miami was in the midst of responding to the Zika outbreak), affordable housing and sea level rise.

During the strategy development phase of Resilient305, key university representatives from Florida International University, University of Miami, and Miami Dade College provided input in collaborative cross-sector stakeholder gatherings, initially at a large kick-off convening and then later as CROs convened stakeholder groups in specific areas of interest (e.g., housing, transportation, youth and education, planning, environment) and then as they again brought specific groups together to do a deeper discovery of issues and possible interventions. This process built relationships and understanding of expertise and interests, strengthening a social network that is quicker to respond to new challenges and opportunities.

Participatory engagement and future visioning through UREx and other NSF programs

In 2015, FIU received funding to work in collaboration with the 12 city-university network, the UREx SRN. FIU's city partnership began with Miami Beach and evolved to include more significant participation of the City of Miami. The goal of this research was to co-produce among academics and practitioners a social, ecological, and technological framework for building urban resilience in the face of climate uncertainty (e.g., Iwaniec et al., 2020). Major activities of the work focused in the Greater Miami and the Beaches region (City of Miami Beach, City of Miami, and Miami-Dade County) and in close partnership with practitioners from these local government entities included a governance knowledge survey (Muñoz-Erickson et al., 2017) and a scenarios workshop. In preparation for the scenarios workshop to help the FIU project team become more acquainted with community dialogue facilitation, we co-hosted a 'World Café' with the City of Miami, held at Ventures Café (a regular small-business expo and community knowledge exchange). An NSF Smart and Connected Communities (SCC) planning grant supported deepened engagement in the form of a series of Community Dialogues. The SCC grant endeavored to co-produce a socio-technological decision-support interface based on adaptation approaches. The integration of work between the UREx SRN and SCC enabled an on-ramp to novel and important ideas that helped set the stage for years of work that followed.

Two major activities of the UREx SRN required in-depth practitioner–academic engagement (e.g., governance survey) and co-production (e.g., scenarios workshop). The governance survey was broadly distributed and received 100 responses from across government, NGO, private sector, and academic sectors. The scenarios workshop was informed by overarching themes identified by the governance survey. The workshop included 40 participants that developed visions for transformative adaptation among distinctive themes of: (1) Adaptation to Compound Flooding, (2) Economic Prosperity and Justice, (3) Smart and Connected City, (4) Eco-City and Food Systems, and (5) Adaptation to Extreme Heat.

FIU support to the development of Miami's first climate adaptation plan

In late 2018, Chief Resilience Officer Jane Gilbert was gearing up to create a comprehensive climate adaptation plan for the City of Miami. She needed improved vulnerability mapping capability and support in her community outreach efforts and reached out to Dr. Tiffany Troxler to see if FIU could potentially be of assistance. Creating the MOU for intern and faculty assistance between FIU and the City of Miami took time as both parties had many other competing demands on their attention and internal processes for vetting the MOU. However, FIU Sea Level Solutions Center, brokered by Dr. Tiffany Troxler, was first able to find a graduate intern to work with the FIU GIS department in the creation of a series of data layers and visual mapping tools that were produced at a neighborhood scale. Second, Dr. Troxler identified a strong undergraduate intern to support the city in organizing a series of neighborhood outreach meetings. Our goal was to maximize participation and to attract a mix of residents from a couple of different neighborhoods in each meeting. This involved a lot of logistics as we sought to provide food, translation services, and childcare and leveraged city and community-based organization networks to recruit people to attend. At each meeting, we were able to share the visual mapping of the impacts of sea level rise and storm surge under different future emission scenarios and of the Landsat surface temperature differentiation indicating areas of higher urban heat island within their neighborhoods. The City Resilience Team and FIU intern facilitated small table-level discussions, and these visuals were able to help spur comments about what residents were experiencing now and most concerned about in the future. The FIU intern also assisted with notetaking and synthesis of ideas and recommendations for building adaptive capacity at the neighborhood and citywide scale. The information gathered at these meetings influenced the prioritization and design of some of the interventions within the Miami Forever Climate Ready Strategy released in early 2020.

Outcomes

The MetroLab Network partnership has evolved into the *Resilient305* Collaborative (Troxler et al., 2021). The *Resilient305* Collaborative was launched in 2019 as an outcome of a MetroLab Network partnership initiated in 2016. The collaborative is a joint academic–government research partnership among Florida International University, Miami-Dade College, University of Miami, and government and non-government organization leaders of GM&B committed to advancing community resilience. The work of the collaborative supports the implementation of Action 49: Collaborate with universities of the Resilient305 Strategy and broadly supports Thrive305. This is a unique partnership which positions GM&B to continue to lead in preparing for and addressing current and future shocks and stressors.

The *Resilient305* Collaborative is piloting a resilience research strategy and monitoring program, focused on an area of GM&B referred to as the 'Little River to North Beach Resilience District' (Figure 4.2). The district is representative of the character of our GM&B community, which makes the lessons learned replicable in other communities throughout GM&B. This diverse area spans communities with varying degrees of exposure to climate hazards, socioeconomic conditions, and technological capacities (e.g., broadband availability, access to sewer). The research strategy will help quantify the benefits of projects, programs, and policies resulting from the ongoing implementation of the *Resilient305* Strategy. Lessons learned from this project will be leveraged to report on and enhance resilience outcomes over time. It will also develop new information to improve the translation of the *Resilient305* Strategy to help meet the resilience priorities of this community and others throughout GM&B. The work would not be possible without the support and partnership with local governments and has now achieved new sources of external support from National Oceanic and Atmospheric Administration's (NOAA) Climate and Societal Interactions (CSI) Division – Adaptation Sciences (AdSci) Program Advancing Climate Adaptation and Coastal Community Resilience.

Overall, we identified ten key outcomes that emerged resulting from four areas of collaboration presented in Table 4.1.

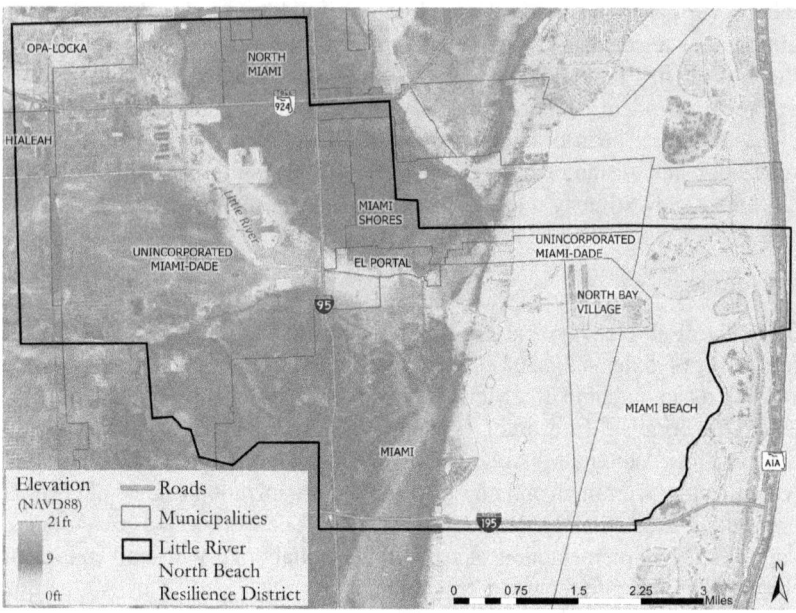

Figure 4.2 The Little River to North Beach (LRNB) Resilience District.

Table 4.1 Ten key outcomes of four areas of collaboration.

1	Enhanced community outreach by both municipality and university
2	Stronger relationships, understanding, trust, and collaborative capacity between different municipalities, college, and universities and between the two.
3	Cost and time saving by sharing of assets such as communication channels, venues for hosting events, staff, and students.
4	Practical learning opportunities and professional connections for students
5	Development of stronger future workforce in the field of urban resilience
6	Creation of shared metrics for monitoring resilience
7	Increased public awareness of current impacts of sea level rise
8	Increased hyperlocal data on tidal flooding
9	Creation of communication and decision-making tools for government officials and residents.
10	New funding for multi-institutional projects focused on collaborative approaches and gaps illuminated in the co-evolution of the resilience collaboration

Reflections

Barriers and obstacles

Universities and municipalities are large institutions with multilayered decision-making and administrative systems so development of formal partnerships can take time.

The end products of research at a university are different than those for a municipality. For instance, the UREx visioning process took more time to define a final product to be shared beyond the city practitioners and university partners involved in directly organizing it than what is expected of city product timelines. This could be because university outputs (e.g., research papers) are often different than what municipalities need for outputs (e.g., PowerPoint presentations, websites, decision tools). It would have been helpful for all parties to have an agreed on a timeline for a final product and audience from the outset.

Both the City of Miami's Office of Resilience and FIU's Sea Level Solutions Center are charged with working both across departments internally and cross-sectorally. However, some of the biggest obstacles were when the Miami CRO and FIU director attempted to get our partner departments to work together as was the case with the City's Information Technology Department and FIU's GIS team. Specifically, City's Office of Information Technology was not able to provide the support to the partnership to work with the FIU data and GIS specialist to assist with the integration of the data platforms within the city systems.

Benefits and enablers

The city was able to get data visualization tools and support with community outreach and documentation at a lower cost and shorter timeframe than had they had to procure this assistance through a competitive process. FIU students and faculty gained a firsthand insight into both how the city works and its constituent engagement processes. With each engagement, the process for collaboration became a bit easier as each side understood organizational parameters and capacities from the outset.

The strengths of this collaboration include that the interns gained invaluable, practical on-the-ground experience of working with local government as well as professional contacts. The city gained support for the development of data tools and outreach activities that it would not have been able to afford or procure through the private sector in a timely manner.

Recommendations and advice

The Miami CRO, Jane Gilbert, and FIU Director of Sea Level Solutions Center, Tiffany Troxler, had both a strong commitment to the collaboration and willingness to adapt to each institutional constraints and capacity. Without this, the collaboration would not have happened. Establishing shared goals, timelines, and specific outcomes from the outset, in addition to investing time in clear, focused, consistent, and frequent communication, are essential to developing a strong and productive working relationship.

Developing an agreement for exchange of climate information and capacity that is mutually beneficial is highly recommended. The student internship agreement developed between the city and FIU enabled a student to work inside government, gain firsthand experience in a local government resilience office, participate in community outreach, and apply university-developed information not otherwise readily available to the city. A second student worked out of the university to support the development of that information applied by the city in community outreach activities. We recommend taking this to the next level by developing an agreement that supports a cohort of students that can work on both sides of the collaboration, to also exchange experiences and skills, complemented by student training and professional development opportunities.

Notably, leveraging the value-add brought by local government–university collaboration that supports student training while also co-delivering high-quality products enables a sustaining relationship with significant additional benefits that may not be immediately quantifiable. To take that step forward beyond the status quo, for instance, as compared with outsourcing work to very large, often non-local consulting firms, is a hallmark of overcoming barriers and engaging in new innovations that reinvest in our community and advance climate solutions that deliver homegrown resilience dividends. Ideally, an ongoing partnership is established that is written into both organizations' budgets and strategic plans. The next step would be to engage higher-level decision-makers to establish this as an annual program with the specific tasks to evolve over time.

Next steps for this work

The Resilient305 Collaborative has the potential to and has already resulted in many more collaborations. For instance, the Sea Level Solutions Day has led to the formation of a new citizen science initiative around urban heat islands called Shading Dade. Additionally, a group of faculty, students, community-based organizations, and municipal and other government agency practitioners have formed an Urban Heat Research Group to share resources, articulate research and data needs, and collaborate on grant applications. We are working toward integrating university-led monitoring and evaluations of municipal-led initiatives and projects. This requires new funding streams that would fund both the projects and their evaluation that are now coming to fruition.

Acknowledgments

We would like to acknowledge the support of the National Oceanic and Atmospheric Administration (NOAA) Climate and Societal Interactions (CSI) Division – Adaptation Sciences (AdSci) Program, Advancing Climate Adaptation and Coastal Community Resilience, The National Science Foundation (NSF) S&CC Program Grant No. CNS1737626 and SRN Program Grant No. SES-1444755, the Miami-Dade County Environmental Education Program Grant No. 19E-FIUF, a Signature Resilience Grant from The Miami Foundation, and a City of Miami-FIU student internship program. We are also grateful for partnerships with Miami-Dade County, City of Miami, City of Miami Beach, the University of Miami, and Miami-Dade College. We also appreciate the support of the Venture Café and The Miami River Commission for the use of their facilities for community workshops. This is contribution # 1435 from the Institute of Environment at Florida International University.

References

Fedler, T. (2009). The economic impact of recreational fishing in the everglades region. *Prepared by Bonefish and Tarpon Trust for the Everglades Foundation*, Palmetto Bay, Florida. Retrieved from www.bonefishtarpontrust.org/downloads/research-reports/stories/everglades-economics-report.pdf

Greater Miami Convention and Visitors Bureau (GMCVB). (2019). *Research and statistics*. Retrieved from www.miamiandbeaches.com/gmcvb-partners/tools-resources/research-statistics-reporting

Hallegatte, S., Green, C., Nicholls, R. J., & Corfee-Morlot, J. (2013). Future flood losses in major coastal cities. *Nature Climate Change, 3*, 802–806. https://doi.org/10.1038/nclimate1979

Iwaniec, D. M., Cook, E. M., Davidson, M. J., Berbes-Blazquez, M., Georgescu, M., Kraysenhoff, E. S., Middel, A., Sampson, D. A., & Grimm, N. B. (2020). The co-production of sustainable future scenarios. *Landscape and Urban Planning, 197*, 103744. https://doi.org/10.1016/j.landurbplan.2020.103744

McCormick, B., Clement, R., Fischer, D., Lindsay, M., & Watson, R. (2010). Measuring the economic benefits of America's Everglades' restoration. *Prepared by Mather Economics for the Everglades Foundation*, Palmetto Bay, Florida.

Muñoz-Erickson, T. A., Miller, C., & Miller, T. M. (2017). How cities think: Knowledge co-production for urban resilience and sustainability. *Forests, 8*, 203. https://doi.org/10.3390/f8060203

Resilient 305. (2019). *Our research*. Retrieved August 8, 2021, from https://resilient305.com/our-research/

Southeast Florida Regional Climate Change Compact Sea Level Rise Work Group (Compact). (2019). Unified sea level rise projection for Southeast Florida. *A Document Prepared by the Southeast Florida Regional Climate Change Compact Ad Hoc Work Group*. Retrieved from https://southeastfloridaclimatecompact.org/wp-content/uploads/2020/04/Sea-Level-Rise-Projection-Guidance-Report_FINAL_02212020.pdf

Troxler, T. G., Clement, A. C., Arditi-Rocha, Y., Beesing, G., Bhat, M., Bolson, J., . . . Wheaton, E. (2021). A system for resilience learning: Developing a community-driven, multi-sector research approach for greater preparedness and resilience to long-term climate stressors and extreme events in the Miami metropolitan region. *Journal of Extreme Events, 8*. http://dx.doi.org/10.1142/S2345737621500196

US Census Bureau. (2010). *American community survey 1-year estimates*. Retrieved July 1, 2020, from data.census.gov. https://data.census.gov/cedsci/

5 Operational guidelines for the identification of green infrastructure in a semiarid city

*Agustin Robles-Morúa,
Eduardo Hinojosa-Robles,
Javier Navarro-Estupiñán,
Diana Meza Figueroa,
Efrain Vizuete Jaramillo &
María G. Peñúñuri*

Introduction

As with other Latin American countries, Mexico has experienced a rapid and accelerated expansion of most of its urban centers. According to the Mexican National Population Council, in 2018, 74.2% of the population lived in cities (92.7 million), which is 2.1% higher than in comparison to 2010. Currently, there are 74 metropolitan areas in which an estimated 84.5% of the population are concentrated. Of these, the top ten largest cities are growing at an alarming rate that ranges between 2% and 3% per year (CONAPO, 2018). To deal with the rapid urban expansion and population growth in the cities, the Secretariat of Territorial and Urban Agrarian Development (SEDATU), in collaboration with the Secretariat of Environment and Natural Resources (SEMARNAT), has been planning and seeking the implementation of climate protection policies, strategies, and measures in Mexican urban policy.

One of the lines of action identified within the urban planning component is Green Infrastructure (GI), which has been seen as an element with the potential to trigger holistic planning, due to its integrating nature of at least four urban functions: water management, mobility, public space, and biodiversity. Additionally, GI becomes a viable option that promotes diverse urban ecosystem services such as climate regulation, pollutant capture, air quality improvement, flood regulation, carbon capture, and support for greater plant cover, and can contribute to groundwater recharge in local aquifers.

DOI: 10.4324/9781003208723-5

68 *Agustin Robles-Morúa et al.*

Different cities in Mexico have sought out resources to finance and conduct their own planning and implementation of strategies to seek nature-based solutions such as GI. In this chapter, we describe a collaborative approach for co-generating knowledge between researchers and practitioners in Hermosillo, a city in northwest Mexico. The synergistic effort helped strengthen collaborations between researchers and practitioners and resulted in a new interdisciplinary way of understanding the problems and the potential solutions. It resulted in a better understanding of the various urban environmental problems affecting the city which allowed for a set of strategies for future interventions.

Description of the case study area

The city of Hermosillo is located in the Sonoran Desert in northwest Mexico (Figure 5.1). It is the capital of the state of Sonora and the center for most of the industrial growth and development in the region. It has an estimated population of 936,263 (INEGI, 2020) with a growth rate of 2% per year since 2010, which is higher than the annual state and national averages (CONAPO, 2018). The city has an impervious cover of 60% (Navarro-Estupiñan et al., 2020), higher than cities in arid climates in the United States, such as Las Vegas, Nevada (40%), and Phoenix, Arizona (45%), as reported by Myint et al. (2015). Hermosillo is ranked third in the nation in its population growth and urban expansion over the past decade.

Over the past five years, several local researchers, primarily from the University of Sonora (UNISON), the Technological Institute of Sonora (ITSON), the College of Sonora (COLSON), and the Sonora State University (UES) have conducted various studies with the aim of characterizing urban-related environmental problems. These studies brought to the attention of municipal government officials that the city has various serious environmental problems, primarily related to air quality with high levels of suspended particulate matter (Meza-Figueroa et al., 2016, 2020) and a higher incidence of respiratory diseases (Ortega-Rosas et al., 2020). The city lacks a vehicular emission control program, and as a result, vehicles circulate without verifying the effective operation of catalytic converters. Additionally, Navarro-Estupiñan et al. (2018 and 2020) documented the impacts of heat waves and heat islands on the city inhabitants. In addition to these challenges, the city also lacks a storm water drainage system and is often affected by urban floods as a result of the monsoonal regime that is responsible for 70–75% of the rainfall during the summer months of July, August, and September (Navarro-Estupiñan et al., 2018).

Through the Municipal Institute of Urban Planning (IMPLAN), other studies were also conducted to better understand the extent of the urbanization

Operational guidelines for the identification of green infrastructure 69

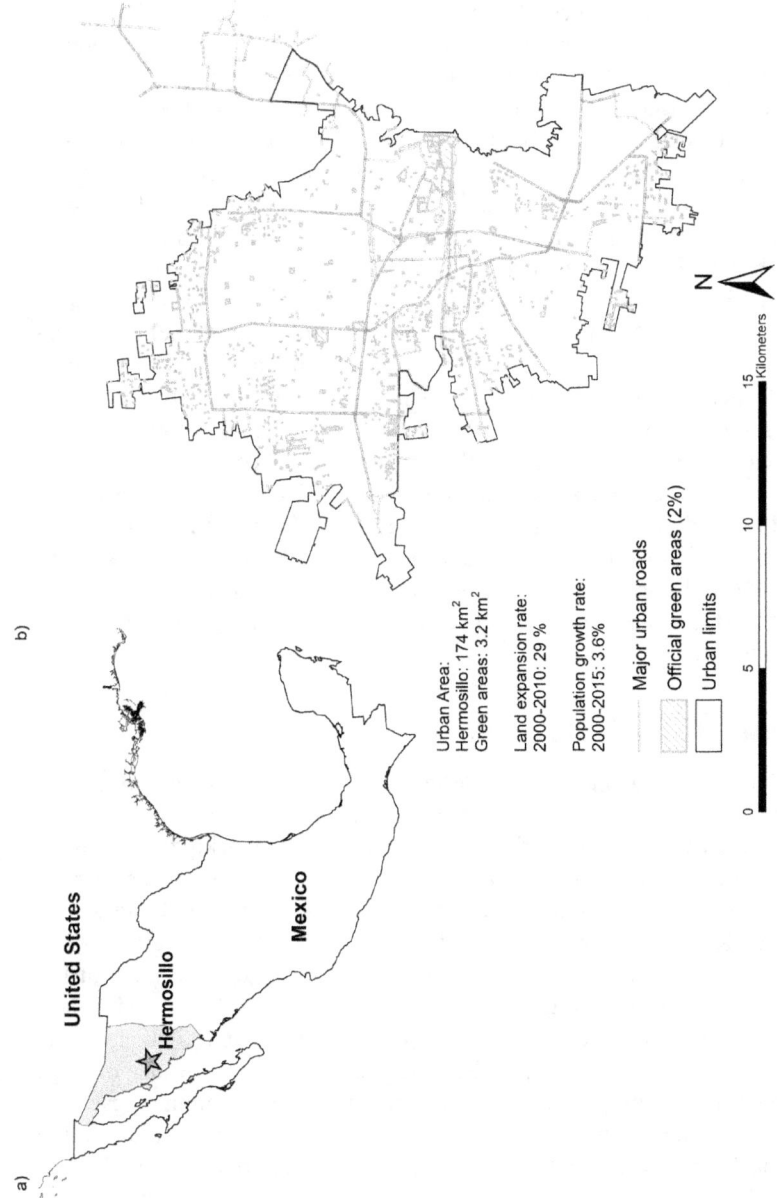

Figure 5.1 (a) Location of the city of Hermosillo, Mexico; (b) Official areas designated as green spaces within the city limits. Source: Instituto Municipal de Planeación Urbana (IMPLAN), 2016.

problem. The city has shown an urban growth typical of cities in the United States of America, with a sprawling and low-density characteristic. Since the 1950s, the city experienced a booming urban expansion, showing its highest growth from 1950 to 1960, with a 120% increase both in urban area and in population (IDB, 2018). By the year 2000, the city had an urban footprint of more than 11,000 hectares with a density of 54 people per hectare (p/ha). This density has been almost consistent in the past 30 years, nowadays being 53.4 p/ha, with a current urban area of over 17,000 ha (IDOM, 2017).

The rapid urban growth of the city has not been consistent with its supply of public space and green areas. It is estimated that green areas within the urban fabric amount to roughly 1,080 ha, whereas peri-urban green areas, part of a land use determined as ecological conservation, sum almost 10,764 ha (IMPLAN, Programa de Desarrollo Urbano-PDU del Centro de Población de Hermosillo 2022, to be published). In total numbers, this supply of open public space might seem fair; however, the distribution and accessibility for the inhabitants in general are not optimal. Another characteristic of the green open space in the city is its lack of connectivity with the natural areas in the outskirts of the urban area, which limits the dispersal of wildlife. In addition, there is a clear preference in the use of foreign species for the greening of the city. Vazquez and Navarro (2016) found that more than 80% of the species used in sidewalks and front yards were introduced, and out of these, only ten species accounted for more than 59% of the specimens identified.

Rationale for doing this work

As mentioned before, the city of Hermosillo is facing several environment-related challenges as well as significant operational issues because the city's infrastructure is old and in some parts of town is lacking. There is no urban drainage system per se; the city uses a 'street-canal drainage' system that puts more stress on the existing water distribution network and wastewater collection system. Newer sections of the city have integrated open storm water drainage systems, but these are very limited and most of the city continues to rely on the streets to move urban runoff. Likewise, it is affected by the North American monsoon circulation pattern, which generates high-intensity rainfall episodes during the summer that cause damage to infrastructure and public health. According to regional climate research, extreme weather events are expected to intensify in the near future in the semi-arid regions of northwestern Mexico and the southwestern United States (Robles-Morua & Garatuza-Payan, 2015). These climatic challenges will be magnified due to the problems associated with rapid urbanization that the city has been experiencing over the past two decades.

To solve these problems and plan for the future, Hermosillo has been working on the development of Municipal Plans for the Adaptation and Mitigation of Climate Impacts, as well as initiatives to collaboratively redesign and evaluate the way in which urban growth is taking place. These strategies have been led locally by the IMPLAN. For these reasons, the city was selected to be part of the Urban Resilience to Extremes Sustainability Research Network (UREx SRN), a US National Science Foundation research project focusing on helping cities find more resilient solutions to the challenges posed by climate change. The municipal government has also been implementing initiatives and seeking additional funding to conduct studies. The city was selected to receive funding by the Ministry of the Environment, Nuclear Safety and Protection of Nature, which commissioned the Deutsche Gesellschaft für Internationale Zusammenarbeit (GIZ) GmbH (German Cooperation for Sustainable Development in Mexico) to conduct studies that would help cities promote more sustainable growth.

The UREx SRN and GIZ efforts were led by local researchers working alongside city officials and urban planners with the goal of generating information that is useful for the development of an updated urban planning program for the city. This would ideally allow solutions that transcend beyond the political term of elected officials. Researchers from the Technological Institute of Sonora (ITSON) coordinated both projects. In addition to these academic and practitioner interactions from the UREx and GIZ projects, IMPLAN in collaboration with the Inter-American Development Bank (IDB) conducted the study 'Vulnerability and Natural Risks in Hermosillo' (IDOM, 2017), which was financed by the North American Development Bank (NADBANK) under the Emerging and Sustainable Cities Program in order to assess the vulnerability to climate change and disaster risk for the city.

In these three projects (UREx SRN, GIZ, and IDB), the city was selected because there were already several research groups focused on analyzing urban problems that relate extreme weather events and public and environmental health issues. These projects came together at the right time and allowed for very rich interactions between experts from various disciplines and city planners.

Details of what was done

The three projects mentioned before were conducted in close collaboration with municipal authorities (IMPLAN) and included different mechanisms for interactions (Figure 5.2). Multiple one-on-one meetings between researchers and the directors of municipal agencies and their staff with responsibilities directly tied to urban planning took place, primarily with

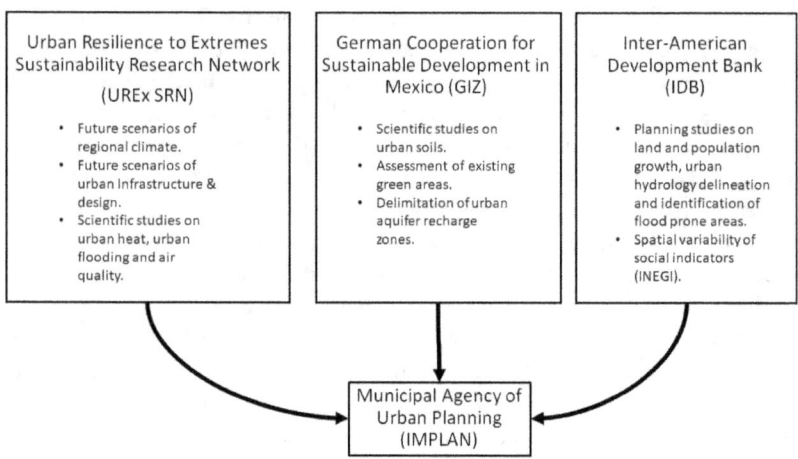

Figure 5.2 Chart of activities that occurred across the three projects: UREx SRN, GIZ, and IDB.

IMPLAN. In addition, several workshops and training sessions were conducted. For example, as part of the UREx project, two future scenarios workshops were conducted with city officials and representatives from various civil and private organizations. These scenarios workshops laid a foundation of the goals and expectations for the city of the future. These workshops also allowed for a clear dissemination of existing academic research studies and were able to translate them into practical information to be incorporated in the strategies developed by city officials, all of this with feedback from representatives from the civil society. The IDB project also allowed for multiple interactions with members from the civil society through workshops that sought feedback on the more problematic issues affecting citizens.

Another kind of collaborative interaction took place in the form of training sessions, where detailed spatial analysis techniques were presented to help city planners better understand the location of areas with more vulnerability to various urban-related environmental problems. These training sessions resulted in reports that were presented to the city officials (directors) and a selected group of stakeholders for feedback. The result of these interactions led to the development of a single-score vulnerability or ecological services map that represented the most problematic areas where IMPLAN could prioritize its efforts and the implementation of pilot projects for GI.

Similarly important, as part of the UREx project, internships of undergraduate and graduate student researchers participating in both the UREx and GIZ projects led to a strengthening of the synergistic activities being conducted. This collaboration also instilled in researchers a sense of urgency to get immediate practical results for city officials, instead of the usual, longer time period typical of academic research and theses. These internships had a two-sided benefit: students interacted with technicians working on real urban planning issues, and city planners were exposed to new techniques that students had learned in the classroom.

Many specific tasks and products were created and are summarized in the following text. For most of these tasks, spatial maps were created and integrated using a hot spot clustering technique, which can generate a map with a single combined score. The clustering analysis was led by researchers at the Technological Institute of Sonora following the procedures described in Navarro-Estupiñan et al. (2020). The final product was developed in a three-day workshop with city planners. Data preparation and processing for the hot spot analysis layers were created in previous training sessions with city officials, using products generated mainly from the research projects mentioned earlier and previous efforts conducted by IMPLAN. The single-score vulnerability map, which was generated using multiple other spatial layers, represents an example of the outcome of the collaborative work between the academics and practitioners.

Table 5.1 summarizes the layers used to create the single-score vulnerability map. Every layer that was used in the clustering map was normalized from 0 to 1, where 1 being the areas that have the highest scores and most vulnerable to the environmental and social problems that can be addressed using GI. In addition to the vulnerability map, urban planners requested that every existing green area be ranked according to where it is located on the vulnerability map. This ranking or prioritization map represents the ecosystem services that are provided by existing green areas, in the sense that they are helping to ameliorate the environmental problems contained in the vulnerability map. In addition, the research team and IMPLAN invited technicians from other agencies to provide feedback and participate in the generation of certain layers. For example, analysts from the Statistics and Geography Agency (INEGI) were invited to help provide more detailed information on spatially explicit social vulnerability and marginalization indicators. INEGI experts also collaborated in the generation of a map that describes the potential areas for aquifer recharge. Similarly, technicians from the local, state, and federal water management agencies provided input on climate scenarios that were developed using local ground observations and remote sensing and modeling products.

Table 5.1 Description of the layers co-generated between academics and practitioners to develop a single-score vulnerability map that helps identify areas of priority for future public spending on green infrastructure.

Layer Name	Characteristics	Outcomes Associated with This Layer
Flood zones	Two types of flood zone maps were merged together: (1) An official version developed by IMPLAN in collaboration with a consulting agency using the rational method and historical knowledge of areas that flood in the city; (2) a flood zone map developed by the IDB using the depression areas that could be filled with a 20-year return period rainfall event (blue spots).	A 2-D hydrologic-hydraulic model was developed, and although this was not incorporated, it is a new tool that city planners have available. The model requires better information to be calibrated. Researchers and practitioners are working together to establish 'experimental' urban watersheds where measurements and monitoring will need to be conducted to calibrate this type of modeling tools.
Atmospheric particles deposition (dusts)	Using the results of the studies of the medical geology research group led by Dr. Diana Meza Figueroa, distribution maps of the concentrations of Calcium (Ca), Chromium (Cr), Iron (Fe), Lead (Pb), and Copper (Cu) were generated in mg kg^{-1}. The maps are the result of a monitoring study using a network of 35 points, located in public schools (Meza-Figueroa et al., 2016). Dust samples were taken before (pre-monsoon) and after (post-monsoon) the summer rainy season. Interpolation methods (kriging) were used to identify areas with a higher concentration of heavy metals and compared against background values for each mineral. Each of the maps of the spatial distributions of heavy metal concentrations were integrated to generate a single map of exposure to environmental (atmospheric) pollution in Hermosillo. The integrated map of heavy metals found in dust was created using the 'worst quantile' tool, which consists of extracting the value of each of the pixels and based on the concentration of the analyzed metal. Two normalized maps were created to indicate the presence of metals in the pre-monsoon and post-monsoon periods.	The various studies providing information on the exposure to potentially toxic elements (PTEs) resulted in the launching of a citywide effort to monitor air quality and improve the existing infrastructure of air quality monitoring stations. Currently, the city has only one station that provides weekly information on air quality. City officials in collaboration with researchers have written several proposals to fund and implement a larger number of monitoring sites, particularly in areas that are already known to have high deposits of dust with PTEs. This monitoring program is intended to become an early warning system for air pollution and extreme heat.

Operational guidelines for the identification of green infrastructure 75

Heat island map	Several efforts have taken place to better understand the impacts of extreme heat in the city. Two stand out because they were developed in close collaboration with technicians from the urban planning agency. The first is a summer campaign using air temperature sensors mounted on vehicles to generate diurnal estimates of heat maps across the city. The second was a heat risk (thermal) map that was generated using remote sensing images of surface temperature from the Landsat 8 satellite in a period of time from March 2013 to December 2017. This second effort was further analyzed by the academic team to explore the spatial and temporal variability of surface temperatures through a statistical stability technique based on the average relative difference and the mean square error of the relative difference. This methodology was used in the research work of Navarro-Estupiñan et al. 2020, obtaining as a result a thermal map that was also normalized to be used in the clustering technique. This map and the results of the heat wave study using existing climate stations in the city were used to develop a series of infographics warning citizens in specific neighborhoods and providing suggestions on how to cope with extreme temperatures during heat wave episodes.	The most immediate outcome is the incorporation of heat vulnerability maps in planning documents and citywide communication campaigns and neighborhood-specific infographics warning about the public health impacts of extreme heat. In addition, a city ordinance was issued (pre-COVID-19) that all public buildings will be used as shelters during heat wave episodes. Similar to the air pollution studies, the extreme heat studies, being conducted in collaboration between academics and practitioners, are an ongoing effort. The plan is to develop an early warning system using air temperature sensors deployed in a larger number of neighborhoods.
Heat social vulnerability map	A map using five indicators of vulnerability associated with deaths caused by extreme heat was identified by Dr. Rolando Díaz-Caravantes and colleagues from the College of Sonora (COLSON). These indicators were further analyzed with analysts from INEGI and IMPLAN, and an additional five infrastructure indicators were included to generate a normalized extreme heat social vulnerability map. This map uses the statistically significant areas defined by INEGI (AGEBs) to show spatial variability in the city of different social indicators.	These 10 indicators were normalized and multiplied with the heat risk (thermal) map to obtain a normalized heat risk map that incorporates physical exposure to heat and social vulnerability associated with extreme heat. The final product was used in the development of the single score hot spots clustering technique. This product and the most vulnerable areas are highlighted in the urban planning program that will be released in 2022 by IMPLAN.

(Continued)

Table 5.1 (Continued)

Layer Name	Characteristics	Outcomes Associated with This Layer
Aquifer recharge zones	In collaboration with geology experts from the National Institute of Statistics and Geography (INEGI). A gravimetric model was used to estimate the depths of the basement of the city's aquifer. The estimates were obtained through the principle of a gravimeter, which allows knowing the difference in gravity that exists at different points on the earth's surface. The result of the gravimeter is a qualitative map of the depths of the basement, which, when related to the depths obtained from the lithological profiles of the wells in the city, allows for the estimation of a quantitative map with depths in meters.	Although the results of the gravimetric model are very coarse, it provides estimates of the locations that are more suitable for aquifer recharge. As a result of this work, more detailed studies are being conducted to look at the evolution of groundwater levels in the urban aquifer. This has been done in collaboration with academics, IMPLAN, and the local water agency.

Operational guidelines for the identification of green infrastructure 77

Feasibility map for the location of green infrastructure

In order to clarify the potential areas that are more suitable for the implementation of green infrastructure, during the meetings and workshops with urban planners and their technicians two schemes were considered. First, we identified areas exclusively based on their ability to recharge the urban aquifer. This included the correlation of flood-prone areas with the areas that are more suitable for recharge based on the depth to bedrock (gravimetric model estimates). On the same map, the centroids of the green areas of the city were superimposed. Since these are the potential sites to implement green infrastructure or expand green areas, each green area site was ranked on the basis of the highest hot spot value obtained. The second scheme included the entire set of environmental and social variables that allowed the identification of multiple ecosystem services (floods, aquifer recharge, heat shock prevention, and reducing air pollution). Researchers and practitioners considered that the reduction of air pollution could occur as dust particles settle in areas that are able to infiltrate water and retain it in soil, and therefore less resuspension of particles could occur. Areas that are vegetated are more likely to promote infiltration and reduce resuspension, whereas impervious surfaces such as streets are most likely to promote the resuspension of dust particles.

With both schemes considered, the hot spot (Getis-Ord Gi*) spatial integration technique was used to generate spatial maps. This allowed the identification of a set of weighted entities with higher values (hot spots) or lower values (cold spots) that are grouped spatially, identifying statistical clusters. This analysis works by finding each feature within the context of neighboring features, so a high value on one feature may not be a statistically significant hot spot as it needs to be surrounded by other features with high values. The local sum of this and its neighbors is compared proportionally with the sum of all entities. When the local sum is very different from the expected one, and that difference is too large to be the result of a random option, a score (z) is considered statistically significant. The larger the value of z, the more intense the cluster of high values (hot spot). Conversely, the smaller the z-score, the stronger the cluster of low values (cold spot).

Results of the integration of all the variables and the ranking of existing green areas showed that there are three large areas where there is a greater cluster of the environmental variables analyzed. These areas are located to the east, west, and northwest of the city. It is worth mentioning that the east of the city is where commercial areas are located, with a considerable flow of inhabitants as the different urban transport lines also converge. This situation makes this area a critical point of attention. Areas to the west and northwest of the city are high and medium-density housing zones, toward which urban sprawl has been growing, with very few spaces designated as green areas.

Outcomes

Changes in urban policies regarding green spaces and green infrastructure

With the objective to advance in the implementation of green infrastructure, the municipality, through IMPLAN, has been working closely with researchers from multiple local universities to incorporate results from scientific studies and co-generating new information. This strategy was aimed to further strengthen and expand the development of green infrastructure. Collaborators intend to do this by establishing new conservation areas and green corridors that integrate a network at a city scale; developing regulations and land value capture instruments to enforce and finance, respectively, the conservation and construction of green infrastructure; and applying a more integrated approach that emphasizes green infrastructure and other sustainability-based measures as the most important tools for mitigation or adapting to climate change.

The collaborative effort between academics and practitioners led to the recent crafting of a coherent public policy that so far is integrated by four policy documents:

1. A design guidelines manual (2017): This provides detailed dimensions and recommendations for various types of GI that can be used at different scales for parking lots, streets medians, sidewalks, roofs, and gardens, among others.
2. A construction code for all real estate developments (2018): This requires the inclusion of green infrastructure in all projects, particularly aimed at implementing sidewalks and medians that allow the capture of some urban runoff. This strategy aims to minimize the velocities of urban runoff and therefore improve the potential for aquifer recharge, and to reduce the inefficiency of the existing street canal drainage used by the city. This strategy is also aimed at promoting the capture of urban sediments in vegetated areas that will result in a reduction of the resuspension of dusts, therefore reducing air pollution.
3. A mandatory vegetation palette (2020): This was developed as a complement to the aforementioned construction code. It identifies specific types of native plants that consume less water, to be used in green areas and green infrastructure projects.
4. The Programa de Desarrollo Urbano (PDU) to be released in 2022: This new urban development plan includes the results that are shown here (with

Operational guidelines for the identification of green infrastructure 79

more details) and is the planning document that will dictate the growth of the city in the next decade. It describes the areas that are more suitable for growth and the areas that need to be protected to maximize environmental benefits within the urban landscape. It also highlights the benefits provided by green infrastructure and is linked to the design of the green infrastructure manual that was released in 2017. To be included in this plan is the city's newly constructed 'sponge city policy.' This resulted directly from the interactions and future scenarios workshops developed by researchers and participating stakeholders during the UREx SRN project.

Classification of priority sites for the construction of green infrastructure

Using the locations of the official green areas (see Figure 5.1.) delimited by IMPLAN, the centroids of each polygon were obtained to extract the z-values of the hot spot map associated with the properties of each ecosystem service. This was done with the purpose of carrying out a priority ranking. The result was a total of 1,870 points, which comprise both 'hot spots' and 'cold spots' distributed around the city. The green areas located in downtown 'parque Madero' obtained the highest score (based on ecosystem benefits), which is a very busy area of the city and also has areas that function as flood zones. This was followed by other smaller green areas located in the downtown area of the city, highlighting the Children's Park, being also an area with a large influx of people and children in particular. Other areas of the city that showed high values in the ranking were Parque La Sauceda and the baseball fields near the main channel of the Sonora River. Also worth noting is the Jardín Juárez, located in the center of the city in an area with high pedestrian transit. Toward the north of the city, there is an important area of 'hot spots'; however, the green areas registered by IMPLAN are smaller than those located in the downtown area.

Toward the west of the city, there is another large area of 'hot spots' with very few land uses such as green areas, being more evident in areas with higher z values. It is worth mentioning that, despite being areas of the city with a lot of development, you can find some lots that have not been developed, which could be used by the city as green areas with a high impact on ecosystem services. In the same way, there are private lots in the area such as schools or sports fields where green infrastructure could be implemented that would provide the ecosystem services in question without affecting their optimal functioning. Coincidently, the first pilot project constructed in the city is located in the west of the city (Figure 5.3). It was implemented in a median in front of the airport's entrance, on one of the busiest streets of the city: Blvd. García Morales. The design was done so that the stormwater that flows through the street was collected in a stream-like basin, which incorporated native plants and mineral

Figure 5.3 Green Infrastructure pilot project built by the municipality in collaboration with Arbol 2000, a local company. (a) Conditions before the project was implemented in 2016; (b) Two years after implementation.

mulch. Artificial irrigation was provided only in the first year after its construction, and since then, all the vegetation has been supported by rainwater.

Reflections

Barriers and obstacles

In terms of the collaborative effort, the team did not find any real obstacles beyond the need to accommodate difficult agendas from elected officials, busy researchers, and directors of municipal and state government agencies.

One aspect of the collaborations that must be highlighted is that directors for all municipal agencies are appointed by the city mayor every three years. If a different party wins the municipal elections, the new directors must be briefed and brought on board with the ongoing efforts. In our collaboration this was exactly the case, but it did not hinder continuing to work together.

Another important obstacle to mention is funding, all of the projects mentioned here were financed from outside sources with little monies allocated from the municipal government for research studies. The funding obtained from the municipal government was used to implement a few pilot test studies. This is an important area that both researchers and practitioners are continuing to work together to secure funding for continuing research projects and construct more green infrastructure throughout the city.

Among the things that are limiting work from the practitioner's point of view was insufficient resources to have a supervising unit at IMPLAN. This unit could work on monitoring whether real estate developments are complying with the new green infrastructure construction policies/code, but resources are insufficient to fully track behavioral changes in accordance with research findings and resulting policies.

Benefits and enablers

This work sought to show how a collaborative effort between a group of academics with different backgrounds worked closely with urban planners to develop spatially explicit products that can help guide future public investments in green infrastructure. The group that collaborated on the three projects described previously is highly interdisciplinary, both academically and also from a practical point of view. For example, researchers from the Environmental Engineering Program at the Technological Institute of Sonora provided great expertise on the use of geographic systems and trained many other researchers and practitioners on how to use them as practical products. To accomplish that, new sets of data needed to be derived. This is where experts from other areas such as the medical geology group from the University of Sonora, or the public health and social sciences group from the College of Sonora, came in to provide feedback and very detailed data from their own studies and knowledge of the city. The academic team was contrasted by a practitioner team that included architects, accountants, civil engineers, ecologists, graphic designers, web developers, communicators, and social workers.

The collaborative process required many meetings, most of them one-on-one, but many group meetings were critical to find a common understanding and learn from each other's knowledge. This also relied on having very crucial information from city planners and technicians working in the urban planning office. Their knowledge of what actually occurs in specific neighborhoods allowed for a better interpretation of the results, and thus provided a reality check on work that was conducted entirely from an academic point of view.

One of the most enriching aspects of the collaboration was the continuous efforts to think about the work that needs to be conducted to improve the quality of the information that is currently available. Although everyone that collaborated feels that a lot was achieved, most considered that more work needs to be done and that we cannot stop here. Both the researchers and practitioners considered that not enough information is available and the products that were created can be improved significantly. The team also discussed the mechanisms for making sure that this information can be integrated into the local norms and urban policies, something that actually is happening as a result of these interactions. Throughout the development of the three projects described here, more government agencies were incorporated, such as the Municipal Institute of Ecology, which has been given the responsibility to oversee the monitoring of air quality in the city and the operation of the city nursery, which now focuses primarily on native species.

Recommendations and advice

Future collaborations between academics and practitioners must continue the ongoing tradition of sharing and co-producing knowledge. As new researchers start new urban-related projects they should reach out to urban agencies, in particular those like IMPLAN, which has been keen to stay informed and obtain all types of urban-related studies.

Similarly, inter-agency collaborations need to be strengthened. With the changes of directors almost every three years, some find it more difficult to take on additional responsibilities in addition to the main purpose of each agency. The more relevant agencies that need to be working together are the planning agency, the water operation and management, the ecology department, the infrastructure and public services and facilities agency, and the office of the city mayor. Other important agencies to consider including in a collaboration are the communications department, the social services and inclusion agency, and the health department.

Next steps for this work

Technically, the collaborations between the academic team and the practitioners sought to integrate the several environmental risks to which the city is exposed and which have not been fully addressed by the authorities, developers, and decision-makers. This also allowed a great opportunity to quantify spatially the ecological benefits of green areas and potential green infrastructure by taking advantage of the natural resources of our environment such as soil, water, and vegetation to counteract the adverse conditions previously described. There are still many things that are underway. Some are more researcher–practitioner collaborations on studies of climate change, air quality, and urban hydrology. From a more conceptual or planning perspective, the team considered the following items as critical for advancing in the implementation of green infrastructure:

- Currently the city has very limited spaces that can be used for new green areas. In that regard, the authorities will need to begin a program for purchasing land within the urban area to be able to increase the vegetation coverage. This is a complicated issue, but practitioners and researchers during the workshops discussed the possibility for accomplishing this via the inclusion of the private sector construction firms and establishing more strict regulations with regard to the amount of green space per square meter in all new buildings.
- The design and implementation of a vast array of greywater reuse infrastructure such as constructed wetlands, laundry to landscape, biofilters, and so on, has not been considered in the new PDU, primarily because

it falls in the jurisdiction of the water facility. However, as the current plan is still under development, several meetings have taken place for the incorporation of a mega infiltration park that will include several of these types of infrastructure.
- Establishing a citizen environmental monitoring and educational program was also considered critical for changing the perceptions regarding green infrastructure and promoting a new culture of seeking alternatives to maximize ecological services at multiple scales in the city.
- Finally, a program with incentives for owners to implement GI at their households or in the sidewalks in front of them is needed as the municipality has very limited funding and will have to rely on private efforts to increase the amount of GI projects.

Additional studies that are needed in no order of relevance are listed here:

- The city has not explicitly included strategies to deal with drought or to plan ahead the role of urban infrastructure in the potential to maximize aquifer recharge in the same way that other cities with similar climate have done (Phoenix and Tucson, USA).
- More detailed scenarios that are spatially explicit in the city on the outcomes and ways to ameliorate climate change need to be incorporated.
- The lack of validation studies of urban runoff volumes as there are no urban gauging stations or stage meters anywhere in the city. The amount of water that flows in the rainwater infrastructure is unknown; the volumes that can be infiltrated to recharge the urban aquifer are also unknown. This was identified as a major potential resource of water, and it would also result in the reduction of costs associated with damages related to street maintenance.
- The lack of detail in the qualitative gravimetric model of the city, specifically as it does not have approximate depths of the basement. As well as the lack of detail of the geology within the urban area. This requires more studies to be conducted at the urban scale. In addition, the lack of periodic monitoring of the static level of the urban and peri urban aquifer needs to be standardized at the same time of year and if possible to have information twice a year to estimate yearly aquifer recharge rates.

Acknowledgments

This research was partially funded by the Urban Resilience to Extreme Events Sustainability Research Network (NUMBER), the German Cooperation for Sustainable Development Agency in Mexico (GIZ Mexico), and the North American Development Bank (NADBANK) through IMPLAN. Team members would like to thank many other staff members (too many to be named here) and technicians from various other municipal government agencies as well as many other researchers and stakeholders that interacted with us and provided valuable feedback.

References

Consejo Nacional de Poblacion. (2018). *CONAPO 2018: Sistema Nacional Urbano.* Secretaria de Gobernacion, Mexico 66 pages. ISBN: 978-607-427-315-1. Retrieved from www.gob.mx/conapo/documentos/sistema-urbano-nacional-2018

IDOM. (2017). *Estudios base: Cambio Climático, Vulnerabilidad, Riesgo Naturales y Crecimiento Urbano en Hermosillo.* Retrieved from www.proyectosmexico. gob.mx/wp-content/uploads/2019/06/Plan-de-acci%C3%B3n-Hermosillo.pdf

Instituto Nacional de Estadistica y Geografia e Informatica. (2020). *INEGI: Resultados del censo de poblacion 2020: Sonora.* Retrieved from www.inegi.org.mx/rnm/index.php/catalog/632

Inter American Deveopment Bank (IDB). (2018). *Rethinking Hermosillo: Through the IDB program: Emerging sustainable cities.* Retrieved from www.implanhermosillo.gob.mx/wp-content/uploads/2018/08/Rethinking-Hermosillo-2017_09_27-Spanish-1.pdf

Meza-Figueroa, D., Barboza-Flores, M., Romero, F. M., Acosta-Elias, M., Hernández-Mendiola, E., Maldonado-Escalante, F., . . . García-Rico, L. (2020). Metal bioaccessibility, particle size distribution and polydispersity of playground dust in synthetic lysosomal fluids. *Science of the Total Environment*, 136481. https://doi.org/10.1016/j.scitotenv.2019.136481

Meza-Figueroa, D., González-Grijalva, B., Del Río-Salas, R., Coimbra, R., Ochoa-Landin, L., & Moreno-Rodríguez, V. (2016). Traffic signatures in suspended dust at pedestrian levels in semiarid zones: Implications for human exposure. *Atmospheric Environment*, *138*, 4–14. https://doi.org/10.1016/j.atmosenv.2016.05.005

Myint, S. W., Zheng, B., Talen, E., Fan, C., Kaplan, S., Middel, A., . . . Brazel, A. (2015). Does the spatial arrangement of urban landscape matter? Examples of urban warming and cooling in Phoenix and Las Vegas. *Ecosystem Health and Sustainability*, 1–15. https://doi.org/10.1890/EHS14-0028.1

Navarro-Estupiñán, J., Robles-Morua, A., Vivoni, E. R., Espíndola-Zepeda, J., Montoya, J. A., & Verduzco, V. S. (2018). Observed trends and future projections of extreme heat events in Sonora, Mexico. *International Journal of Climatology*, *38*(14), 5168–5181.

Navarro-Estupiñan, J., Robles-Morua, A., Diaz-Caravantes, R., & Vivoni, E. R. (2020). Heat risk mapping through spatial analysis of remotely-sensed data and socioeconomic vulnerability in Hermosillo, Mexico. *Urban Climate*, 31. https://doi.org/10.1016/j.uclim.2019.100576

Ortega-Rosas, C. I., Enciso-Miranda, C. A., Macías-Duarte, A., Morales-Romero, D., & Villarruel-Sahagún, L. (2020). Urban vegetation cover correlates with environmental variables in a desert city: Insights of mitigation measures to climate change. *Urban Ecosystems*, *23*(6), 1191–1207.

Robles-Morua, A., & Garatuza-Payan, J. (2015). *Cambio Climático en México: Impactos Esperados en la Disponibilidad del Agua.* Libro editado por la Universidad Nacional Autonoma de Mexico.

Vazquez, J., & Navarro, L. (2016). Cambios en el paisaje arbolado en Hermosillo: escasez de agua y plantas nativas. *Región y Sociedad.* Retrieved from www.scielo.org.mx/pdf/regsoc/v28n67/1870-3925-regsoc-28-67-00079.pdf

6 Community science for the (climate) win

An equity-based framework for understanding and acting on extreme urban heat

Jeremy S. Hoffman, Vivek Shandas & Lara Johnson

Introduction

Human-caused climate change exacerbates existing racial, economic, environmental, and other forms of structural inequality in the United States. Virtually no sector is shielded from the acute effects of climate change, though areas of public health, housing, transportation, and economic vitality are of notable concern (Reidmiller et al., 2018). Urban areas further amplify particular climate stressors like heat (Oke, 1982), rainfall (Shepherd et al., 2002), and air quality (Stone, 2008) through modifications of the surface energy balance due to the buildup of impervious, developed surfaces at the expense of natural landscapes. These climate inequities brought about by urban planning are in some ways sustained and perpetuated by systems that privilege and protect voices that are overrepresented in climate planning and adaptation practice (Leonard, 2021; Wilson, 2020). One potentially transformative approach to equitable governance with respect to climate change is engaging communities in effective climate research models that include their place-based knowledge, interests, and motivations to move from simple awareness to localized action on climate change (either as mitigation or as adaptation) (Bey et al., 2020).

With a few exceptions, current approaches to understanding and acting on climate-induced stressors are highly technical and do little to accommodate place-based considerations and/or community visions in their implementation or execution. Computational models and/or empirical observation rarely, if ever, include active engagement of community members as direct participants in or even recipients of climate data. Moreover, extant climate action planning frameworks largely occur through spatially coarse assessments with relatively limited direct involvement of the community-serving groups and practitioners that they are meant to inform on regional-level assessment scales

DOI: 10.4324/9781003208723-6

(Hamlet et al., 2020; Reidmiller et al., 2018). This lack of locally relevant context, which community members often hold, can severely limit the applicability of research projects that seek to provide data to questions related to the much finer-scale hyperlocal (i.e., at spatial scales finer than a square kilometer) impacts of climate change, such as urban flooding and heat. Without involving community members in the generation of actionable, highly resolved data, current projects limit civic resources going to the highest-need frontline areas, which are known to be hit 'first and worst.' Needed are participatory urban climate knowledge-to-action (PUCKA) frameworks that center historically marginalized communities in assessing those impacts and identifying promising practices at the local scale.

We present here a PUCKA framework through which researchers, practitioners, and public alike can transform their localized climate adaptation potential by producing highly spatially resolved and actionable data, while engaging in evidence-based models of public participation with science at the local level. The outcome of this approach is a 'civically legitimate' (i.e., familiar and understood by local organizations and practitioners) dataset that can be leveraged by the community organizations that were deeply involved in the creation of that dataset, thus sustaining a self-reinforcing system of advocacy and action. We then explain how this framework and resulting engagement approach has sustained a focus on integrating research with practitioners and publics in Richmond, Virginia. This framework was developed and implemented in Richmond by co-authors Hoffman, a researcher employed outside of academia at the Science Museum of Virginia, and Shandas, a researcher and professor affiliated with Portland State University. Co-author Johnson is a practitioner manager at the Virginia Department of Forestry and was engaged in the case study project described herein.

The PUCKA framework

We begin by describing the PUCKA framework as a heuristic to integrate several aspects of the social and biophysical dimensions for improving climate action. Two dimensions address fundamental questions in the climate science field – the level of engagement that researchers have with communities and the robustness of the data generated (Figure 6.1).

To describe the level of community engagement, we rely on a new typology of 'community science' (Charles et al., 2020): the Expert, Community-Engaged, and Relational models of public engagement (Schalet et al., 2020), as well as the evolving definition of public engagement with science (Bell et al., 2017). This can be thought of as a spectrum of levels of community member involvement in the assessment of a stressor from a purely expert model to the highly integrated community-engaged model,

Integrating Urban Heat Data and Community Engagement

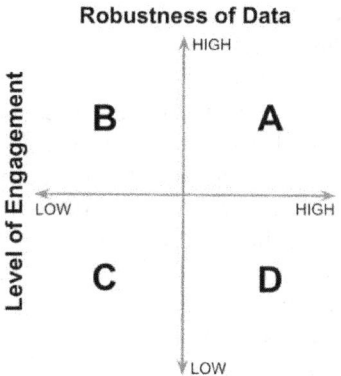

A: People, Place, & Perspective: Consensus on goals, problems, and effective implementation

B: Expert Applications: Specialized knowledge without stakeholder involvement/support

C: Status Quo: Confrontational debate and no improvements

D: Mediated Discussion: Consensus on goals and problems with no help on how to achieve

Figure 6.1 Community engagement and robustness of data framework.

described in the following. We acknowledge that there are no perfect examples of either extreme and that many, if not all, examples of community engagement fall somewhere between these two extremes.

Low levels of community engagement are associated with projects that align closely with the 'expert model' in Schalet et al. (2020). These projects are spearheaded by technical teams of scientists at universities or national laboratories and may 'often carry the expectation that audiences – policymakers, practitioners, and the media – are waiting ready to receive expert knowledge' (Schalet et al., 2020). Our framework's evaluation of a low level of community engagement would be closely aligned with data products that can be accessed from sophisticated online platforms with little or no involvement of the public in their generation or, to a somewhat lesser extent, popular programs in citizen science (Bonney et al., 2016), which are based on a volunteer recruitment and data submission model that is then used by researchers to generate new knowledge about various environmental indicators, with or without the place-based knowledge of the volunteers.

High levels of community engagement in our framework are similar to the community engaged and relational models described in Schalet et al. (2020) and the community science typology presented by Charles et al. (2020). These projects 'emphasize collaboration, reciprocity, respect for local knowledge, community capacity building, and direct intervention in multiple systems of oppression.' which are intertwined with climate change stressors (Charles et al., 2020). This level of community engagement may result in tractable collaborations on new projects in the future. Examples of highly community-engaged projects are reflected in the American Geophysical Union's Thriving Earth Exchange program, which helps scientists, community leaders, and other organizational partners to work together to solve local challenges through collaborative science questioning, designing protocols, implementing the research, and sharing the results (Emerman, 2021).

Reaching high levels of community engagement in climate science research and adaptation practice has several direct and indirect advantages for advancing the climate action and resilience agenda: (1) the co-production of geographically distributed, direct observations of climate phenomena such as heat, precipitation and flooding, air quality, or other variables; (2) building 'civic legitimacy' in climate information and action through socialization of data literacy related to those same stressors; (3) establishing a network or community of practice for cost-effective and robust engagement on climate action and resilience; (4) potential for involving historically marginalized communities in the design, execution, and communication of the findings of the campaigns; and (5) integrating local knowledge that may amplify the goals of several organizations at once, allowing for the data to be leveraged across otherwise disparate organizational missions (e.g., housing and urban agriculture). These are just some of the direct and indirect advantages we have identified through our work on implementing this PUCKA framework.

Data to inform present and future climate stressor changes – produced through highly technical and computationally intensive simulations on Global Circulation Models (GCMs) forced by heat-trapping gas emission/concentration scenarios then 'dynamically downscaled' to region-specific datasets – tend to be coarse in time (months to years) and space (square kilometers), and the current generation of regional climate models show a wide range of possible values for individual stressor changes, with implications for design standards that incorporate climate risk (Cook et al., 2020). These representations of the physical climate system tend to average or smooth out highly complex biogeophysical processes and may not capture the level of granularity that is necessary for local climate action.

Low robustness of data in our framework, then, is the inability to produce and/or implement meaningful interventions that address the stressor at the hyperlocal level; that is, coarse geographic and/or long-duration time scale datasets like gridded climate products and remotely sensed thermal surface information. High robustness of data not only informs knowledge about a particular climate stressor at a high level of detail and precision but also affords the ability to intervene on that stressor at the scale of city blocks or even individual land parcels. These data are highly reproducible and allow for the development of various metrics to show improvement and/or change over time.

The orthogonal superposition of these two dimensions of data robustness and community engagement creates four distinct quadrants, which we evaluate to represent one of four categories of interaction between researchers, publics, and practitioners in the climate adaptation and resilience field:

(A) *People, Place, and Perspective*: Defined by both high levels of engagement and robustness of data, these projects will establish a clear, goal-oriented consensus on the extent of and problems related to the climate stressor's intensity at a hyperlocal level. Moreover, these projects take into account community vision and values to achieve effective implementation of interventions and programming.
(B) *Expert Applications:* Projects in this quadrant are those that use highly robust data but with low levels of community engagement. These projects require highly specialized knowledge and do little to involve stakeholders or support them in obtaining a deep understanding of the data to be used for intervention and implementation.
(C) *Status Quo:* This quadrant identifies projects that make little effort (if any) to work within or with communities or data that can be used in any way to make effective implementation of climate stressor interventions. This ultimately leads to limited or no improvement in the climate stressors' impacts or severity. There may be ongoing and even confrontational debate about whether the stressor is changing, impacting residents, or worth paying attention to in the public sphere.
(D) *Mediated Discussion:* Projects with high levels of community involvement and engagement reach a clear consensus on goals and problems related to climate stressors but may not have the high level of data robustness to achieve effective implementation of interventions.

Programs that recruit, train, and include community members in their methodologies and sustain engagement and application of the findings after the highly robust observations are made within a network of collaborative partnerships define the 'A' quadrant. What follows is a discussion of our application of the PUCKA tenet of *People, Place, and Perspective* to the City of Richmond, Virginia, and its subsequent success as a scaling and building campaign to address extreme urban heat and climate change inequity.

Description of the case study area

Founded on the banks of the James River in 1737, Richmond, Virginia, is a city that is working to heal social, racial, and environmental injustices that are rooted in our nation's Colonial past. Richmond served as both the

Capital of the Confederacy and the United States' second-largest trading port for enslaved persons during the 19th century. Beginning in 1937, 'redlining' practices – the systematic denial of access to home loans, mortgage insurance, or credit based on an applicant's race or ethnicity – prevented the city's predominantly African American neighborhoods from building wealth through homeownership – effectively segregating people of color in less desirable urban neighborhoods that are hotter now than other nearby neighborhoods (Hoffman et al., 2020). Shortly after redlining, Harland Bartholomew authored Richmond's first comprehensive master plan, which would effectively outline the ways that Black-owned and occupied properties would become devalued and determined to be eligible for 'slum clearance.' With no voice in city planning at the time, Richmond's people of color watched as their neighborhoods were damaged or bulldozed wholesale for the construction of highways and the infiltration of factories during Urban Renewal in the decades that followed. Today, the City of Richmond, Virginia, is located in the Eastern Piedmont climate division and is home to over 226,000 residents, making it the fourth most populous city in the Commonwealth. The city still bears the scars of racial segregation as maps of poverty, demographics, income, tree canopy, food access, and vacant property echo privileged investment in wealthier, whiter communities at the expense of Black residents' living conditions.

Rationale for doing this work

In March 2017, the City of Richmond's equity-centered RVAgreen2050 climate action plan was formally announced. This plan was initially focused on reducing Richmond's carbon emissions 80% by 2050 (this goal has since been elevated to net zero by 2050) while also preparing the community for the impacts of climate change. The planning process has continued since, and the formal plan is expected to be adopted by City Council resolution in late 2022.

The city's climate action plan team sought effective datasets to understand their acute exposure to various climate threats. In the Southeast climate region of the United States, these impacts center on increased heat and precipitation extremes for inland urban areas (Carter et al., 2018). The most relevant climate stressors assessed by statewide agencies and researchers at that time included some estimates and context on the health risks of extreme heat but were presented at coarse spatial (county) and long temporal (end-of-century) scales (Steinfeldt et al., 2015). There were no details presented on how urban landscapes may amplify or dampen these large-scale stressors, and little if any attention was paid to describing the disproportionate exposure of frontline communities to extreme heat. A now-defunct local nonprofit organization had summarized National Land Cover Database (NLCD) land cover data (Homer et al., 2015) at the US Census Block Group scale and compared these with the also coarse-scale Moderate Resolution Imaging Spectroradiometer (MODIS) land surface temperatures (Hulley et al., 2018) as well as 2010 Census demographic information. While these initial observations had begun to socialize the idea of extreme heat and the inequitable urban intensification of heat extremes, the coarse scale (~1 kilometer) and non-experiential nature of the available urban heat data for Richmond remained an obstacle for individual- and community-led action on extreme heat interventions at the local level. In fact, these coarse-grained data were often cited as difficult to grasp what exactly would be driving the major patterns in a particular pixel.

Details of what was done

Recognizing the need for data at a more granular and hyperlocal scale to aid the development of the RVAgreen2050 Climate Action Plan, the Science Museum of Virginia, a science and technology center, applied for and received a small research grant from the Virginia Academy of Science to collaborate on a participatory urban heat island assessment campaign employing a recently published technical methodology (Voelkel et al., 2016). This method had used highly detailed observations of air temperature from automobile traverses to model heat surfaces for Portland, Oregon, with remotely sensed land cover data. The authors realized the opportunity to build on this novel methodology, however still largely planned and performed by scientists, by integrating community science (which wasn't a common way to frame this work at the time) into the process. Using this new support alongside existing programmatic focus on the local impacts of climate change from an Environmental Literacy Program award from the National Oceanic and Atmospheric Administration (NOAA) Office of Education (Award #NA15SEC0080009; Hoffman, 2020), the Science Museum of Virginia worked to establish a network of collaborators to participate in the data collection campaign as volunteer community scientists.

This required new partnerships to be developed for the museum, including securing volunteer participation from the employees of the City of Richmond's Office of Sustainability and Department of Planning and Development Review; research support from the University of Richmond's Spatial Analysis Lab and Virginia Commonwealth University's SustainLab; research support from local meteorologists at the Richmond Times-Dispatch and WRIC-TV ABC8; and place-based knowledge in the design and execution of the campaign from Groundwork RVA, a community-based nonprofit working with teens from marginalized neighborhoods to establish and improve access to green spaces in the City of Richmond. This network of partnerships crossed through government, academic, and nonprofit sectors to include organizations whose mission was even tangentially related to acting on extreme urban heat. We all recognized the importance of generating a locally relevant dataset that could be used to prioritize limited resources to maximum effect. The resulting heat data collection effort was known as a 'heat campaign' and captured the *People, Place, and Perspective* tenet of the PUCKA framework as described before.

Once the collaborative partnerships were established (the author admits that many of these began as cold calls and required trust building to maintain), it was time to decide when the campaign would take place. As the urban heat island assessment method we employed (Shandas et al., 2019; Voelkel et al., 2016) uses data collected through three-hour-long vehicular traverses across the study area from vehicle-mounted temperature and global positioning system sensors, there was a need to not only plan for the campaign but also train the volunteer community scientists how to use the technology. First, the research team (Hoffman, Shandas, and a former student) divided the city into sectors that would serve as the basis for the traverse routes ($n = 9$). In collaboration with the partnership organizations, we then identified specific places over which the partners wanted the traverse route to pass, allowing for the place-based knowledge of that particular sector of the city to become incorporated into the campaign methodology.

On the basis of local climatological records of the highest likelihood of a heat event occurrence, the research team targeted the second week of July 2017 for preparing the campaign volunteers. We designed a two-hour campaign orientation session to be held in the evening before the temperature observation traverses were conducted at the Groundwork RVA headquarters in the Six Points Innovation Center, located in a historically marginalized community of color on Richmond's northside. Volunteers were randomly assigned into teams for each vehicle traverse route. These teams may have included youth participants as well as adaptation professional practitioners. This orientation session introduced the volunteer community scientist teams to the physical phenomenon of urban heat islands, outlined the campaign's importance for preparing our city for the impacts of climate change, and gave detailed explanations of and hands-on experiences with the campaign technology. The local meteorologist at the Richmond Times-Dispatch provided the team with weekly updates on the forecast in the lead-up to the campaign. The campaign was initiated after the forecast favored extremely warm temperatures on July 13, 2017 (Boyer, 2017). Volunteer teams were activated, completed the traverses independent of each other, and returned the temperature sensors and GPS units to the analysis team (Figure 6.2). Many of the community scientists remarked that they had interesting conversations about climate change and community engagement within their team's vehicle. In

Figure 6.2 Clockwise from left to right: (a) Community Scientist I'jiana James affixing the mobile thermometer on campaign day, July 13, 2017; (b) Pre-campaign training session for community scientists on July 12, 2017; (c) Sharing the urban heat vulnerability map with VA-04 Congressman Donald McEachin; (d) Co-PIs Hoffman and Shandas developing community scientist team assignments.

addition to alerting the community scientists about the campaign date, we also reached out to several media organizations in Richmond to provide additional press coverage for the campaign. This resulted in considerable public interest and may have contributed to the further socialization of the heat island effect and our data's legitimacy in the public realm.

Outcomes

The Richmond campaign's data, which consisted of over 100,000 temperature observations, revealed an ~15°F difference between the warmest and coolest spots of the city at the same time (3:00 PM) during heat warning conditions (Shandas et al., 2019). Many of the warmest places tended to be within historically marginalized, poorer, and non-white areas throughout the City. These areas also tend to have fewer trees, more imperviousness, less car ownership, lower home ownership rates, poorer health outcomes (including lower life expectancies), and a heavier reliance on public transportation. The coincidence of extreme heat with these socioeconomic variables helped to frame climate change as a social equity issue and not simply an environmental one. Subsequent campaigns coordinated by the authors revealed similar patterns, inspiring a deeper research interest in the historical patterns of these inequitable exposures and environmental conditions (Hoffman et al., 2020). These campaigns have been scaled up to dozens of cities with support from the Climate Resilience Fund and the Climate Program Office at NOAA. In 2021 alone, 27 cities or municipalities participated in a heat mapping campaign based on this framework, 10 of which were in Virginia, and 1 included an update of the 2017 Richmond campaign.

Since 2017, the Richmond collaborative partnership has co-created a set of community-based variables to be included in the construction of a Richmond Urban Heat Island Vulnerability Index (heat, poverty, tree canopy, and imperviousness). While relatively simple, this index correlates well with the distribution of heat-related ambulance responses from the Richmond Ambulance Authority. This index has since been adapted to include dozens of variables and forms the basis of the City of Richmond's RVAgreen2050 Climate Equity Index. In many ways, the collaborative partnerships, which formed our community science campaign, have gone on to galvanize attention on extreme heat events in Richmond. The urban heat and vulnerability maps have been cited in dozens of news articles (googling "Richmond Urban Heat Island" returns several of them from 2020 to 2021 alone); leveraged to marshal millions of dollars in state, federal, and philanthropic support for new projects and initiatives both in Richmond and beyond (Long, 2020); featured in local reports on various aspects of city policy ranging from food security to housing; referenced throughout the Daniel Burnham Award-winning Richmond 300 comprehensive master plan; and are now a centerpiece of an emerging community environmental justice roundtable, which provides feedback for priorities of the RVAgreen2050 plan implementation phase actions, and more. The mayor of Richmond, Levar Stoney, dedicated City resources to establish five new green spaces in the disproportionately impacted southside, representing the largest investment in green space since the 1970s. Perhaps the most exciting outcome of this work has been the local establishment of two nonprofits specifically citing the urban heat island data and their disparity across Richmond in their mission statements.

By including the community organizations that needed this information, in order to advance their missions to achieve meaningful change and climate action, in the design and execution of heat data collection and interpretation, our 2017 collaboration – conducting a heat campaign in accordance with the *People, Place, and Perspective* tenet of the PUCKA framework – has ignited a national and local hunger for this information. Moreover, it has inspired several relevant grant initiatives to retool their approach to fund climate action at the hyperlocal level. One of the most impactful of these is the Urban and Community Forestry Program at the Virginia Department of Forestry. Their reimagination of how to evaluate proposals for tree planting programs has now been used as a model for Federal legislation focused on greening formerly redlined areas of cities like Richmond. The following was contributed by the program's manager, Lara Johnson:

Once the hyperlocal heat and vulnerability data for Richmond were published, several questions came to light: How do we help regreen these specific heat-exposed communities? How do we engage these communities that have largely been treeless for a long time? How do we alleviate resident concerns about trees damaging sidewalks and lack of maintenance? We knew that our typical approach was going to have to change.

The 2017 Richmond campaign's combined work overlaying health-related outcomes, tree canopy, and heat vulnerability helped us reevaluate our internal review of projects in Richmond (and subsequently Norfolk in 2019, and Petersburg beginning in 2022). From a state program manager's point of view, it is so important that we are making sure that we are putting trees where they are needed most and the competitive nature of grant giving can be challenging. We have limited resources and often have more applicants than can be funded, but this heat campaign data help us prioritize social equity as part of our proposal ranking processes. Evidence of community engagement is now required for all grants provided through the urban and community forestry (U&CF) program at the Virginia Department of Forestry. We needed to make sure that projects funded are based on trust with place-based partnerships to help ensure that the community is invested in the trees and their long-term survival. Engaging community members to use the hyperlocal heat data to inform where the trees should go in their eyes is extremely powerful.

This program overhaul led to a pilot partnership with Virginia Commonwealth University Office of Sustainability, Carver Area Civic Improvement League (a neighborhood association near VCU) and Richmond Tree Stewards (a tree advocacy group). Students had been conducting tree inventories as part of class projects, knocking on doors and speaking with residents in the Carver neighborhood about planting trees for many months. Our agency worked with them to develop a tree species list and matched a species to each planting pit. In addition to providing funding for the trees, we used U&CF grant assistance to support maintenance on the project for the tree establishment period. Grant dollars managed by the VCU Office of Sustainability were used to support students going through the 6-week Richmond Tree Steward training and certification program, and they were hired for two summers to help with tree watering in Carver. The Carver Tree Project won a major VCU award in 2019. A similar project based on this model – leveraging the heat data to prioritize tree planting programs – was completed in the Randolph Neighborhood at the Amelia Street School in 2020, and yet another is to be planted in the Historic Jackson Ward Neighborhood in 2021. We provided funding and technical expertise on tree species selection, but it was the place-based partnerships, the hyperlocal data on urban heat, and community engagement that made them successful. I look forward to leveraging other PUCKA framework project data in the future.

Reflections

Barriers and obstacles

Perhaps the most important obstacle we encountered (and continue to encounter to this day) was developing non-extractive, mutually beneficial and non-transactional relationships with the partnership organizations that serve and represent historically marginalized communities. These groups may have been involved in prior project collaborations that did not end in a good place with governmental or academic entities; they may even themselves have lived experience of distrust for institutions. How do we ensure that we're developing these partnerships for the right reasons, and how will we show that our collaboration will meaningfully contribute to their mission beyond the creation of the datasets? One way that we have continued to do this is through co-developing grant proposals and budgets with our partners in a way that provides funding up front instead of as a reimbursement. This has enabled our partners to have an operating budget instead of deficit participation and shows that we value their collaboration and contribution to whatever project is being developed. Of note, we were funded in 2019 by the Institute of Museum and Library Services in collaboration with Groundwork RVA to deepen community science curriculum around air quality and in 2020 by the Office of Education at NOAA to co-develop public engagement materials specific to Richmond's RVAgreen2050 plan. Both of these projects have funded our partner organizations with contracts before any project activities commenced. Moreover, these projects build on the urban heat island assessment campaign and continue to inspire new projects beyond our own.

Benefits and enablers

We view the most important, beneficial aspect of this work to be the intentional building of new, cross-sectoral partnerships and the centrality of an informal science education institution in the development and execution of the campaign. While not necessary to complete the campaign or to apply our framework more broadly, science centers remain one of the most trusted science information sources in the public sphere (Wilkening, 2021). In this case, the Science Museum of Virginia embodied the emerging role of science and technology centers as community climate resilience hubs, bringing together several boundary organizations – that is, groups whose missions closely but maybe not explicitly center on climate change action – into a community science campaign. This, combined with the outcome of such dramatic policy and infrastructural changes, is promising. While many other cities have since undertaken our framework and applied the off-the-shelf service now offered by the CAPA Strategies Heat Watch program (which epitomizes the framework presented in this chapter and is led by co-author Shandas), those that achieve the broadest impact in their local communities are those that incorporate cultural and nonprofit organizations into collaborative efforts and co-creation of their campaigns.

Recommendations and advice

We would strongly recommend that the readers of this book consider how to incorporate non-traditional organizations like science and technology centers or workforce development nonprofits like Groundwork RVA into their research goals and community action. Furthermore, we would stress the importance of adjusting how we compensate and fund community organizations to participate in our programs. Moving from a model whereby community organizations are reimbursed for their participation to one where they are paid for their time up front can alleviate significant pressures that these smaller organizations face in their budgeting and finances. This amelioration of financial pressure can not only benefit the organization itself but also build up trust in the process. Shifting our funding apparatuses to fit this model also requires upstream changes in the funding mechanisms themselves – if federal or philanthropic funding won't allow for this sort of up-front, participatory funding model in the way they require reporting or otherwise, then we must put pressure on these organizations to also shift the way they think about supporting small, community-based organizations.

Next steps for this work

We hope that cultural entities like science and technology centers will continue to develop a local voice for climate action through our framework and focus on urban heat island assessments. We continue to build an evidence base supporting the idea that these community science campaigns advance significant, localized, and strategic climate adaptation interventions. In this way, we hope more communities utilize this framework to advance their own goals. We also suspect that more communities will not only do this campaign framework once but use it as a way to measure the impact of interventions, like here in Richmond, where we have performed our second community science campaign in summer 2021 to understand how large multifamily housing and park investments since 2017 have impacted the patterns of heat exposure in our city.

References

Bell, L., Lowenthal, C., Sittenfeld, D., Todd, K., Pfeifle, S., & Kollmann, E. K. (2017). Public engagement with science. *Creative Commons Attribution Noncommercial-Share Alike*, 77.

Bey, G., McDougall, C., & Schoedinger, S. (2020). *Report on the NOAA office of education environmental literacy program community resilience education theory of change.* https://doi.org/10.25923/MH0G-5Q69

Bonney, R., Phillips, T. B., Ballard, H. L., & Enck, J. W. (2016). Can citizen science enhance public understanding of science? *Public Understanding of Science, 25*(1), 2–16. https://doi.org/10.1177/0963662515607406

Boyer, J. (2017, July 13). Richmond approached triple-digit heat just in time for a study of hot weather. *Richmond Times-Dispatch.* Retrieved from www.richmond.com/weather/richmond-approached-triple-digit-heat-just-in-time-for-a/article_1f0fb2da-7baf-5d6e-bca3-7251b77484ab.html

Carter, L. M., Terando, A., Dow, K., Hiers, K., Kunkel, K. E., Lascurain, A., Marcy, D. C., Osland, M. J., & Schramm, P. J. (2018). *Chapter 19: Southeast: Impacts, risks, and adaptation in the United States: The fourth national climate assessment, Volume II.* U.S. Global Change Research Program. https://doi.org/10.7930/NCA4.2018.CH19

Charles, A., Loucks, L., Berkes, F., & Armitage, D. (2020). Community science: A typology and its implications for governance of social-ecological systems. *Environmental Science & Policy, 106*, 77–86. https://doi.org/10.1016/j.envsci.2020.01.019

Cook, L. M., McGinnis, S., & Samaras, C. (2020). The effect of modeling choices on updating intensity-duration-frequency curves and stormwater infrastructure designs for climate change. *Climatic Change, 159*(2), 289–308. https://doi.org/10.1007/s10584-019-02649-6

Emerman, S. (2021, June 7). Data on your side. *Thriving Earth Exchange Scientist Spotlight*. Retrieved from https://thrivingearthexchange.org/scientist-spotlight-data-on-your-side/

Hamlet, A. F., Byun, K., Robeson, S. M., Widhalm, M., & Baldwin, M. (2020). Impacts of climate change on the state of Indiana: Ensemble future projections based on statistical downscaling. *Climatic Change, 163*(4), 1881–1895. https://doi.org/10.1007/s10584-018-2309-9

Hoffman, J. S. (2020). Learn, prepare, act: "Throwing shade" on climate change. *Journal of Museum Education, 45*(1), 28–41. https://doi.org/10.1080/10598650.2020.1711496

Hoffman, J. S., Shandas, V., & Pendleton, N. (2020). The effects of historical housing policies on resident exposure to intra-urban heat: A study of 108 US urban areas. *Climate, 8*(1). https://doi.org/10.3390/cli8010012

Homer, C., Dewitz, J., Yang, L., Jin, S., Danielson, P., Coulston, J., Herold, N., Wickham, J., & Megown, K. (2015). Completion of the 2011 national land cover database for the conterminous United States: Representing a decade of land cover change information. *Photogrammetric Engineering, 10*.

Hulley, G. C., Malakar, N. K., Islam, T., & Freepartner, R. J. (2018). NASA's MODIS and VIIRS land surface temperature and emissivity products: A long-term and consistent earth system data record. *IEEE Journal of Selected Topics in Applied Earth Observations and Remote Sensing, 11*(2), 522–535. https://doi.org/10.1109/JSTARS.2017.2779330

Leonard, K. (2021). WAMPUM Adaptation framework: Eastern coastal Tribal Nations and sea level rise impacts on water security. *Climate and Development*, 1–10. https://doi.org/10.1080/17565529.2020.1862739

Long, R. (2020, September 15). Formerly redlined areas of Richmond are going green. *Save the Bay*. Retrieved from www.cbf.org/blogs/save-the-bay/2020/09/formerly-redlined-areas-of-richmond-are-going-green.html

Oke, T. R. (1982). The energetic basis of the urban heat island. *Quarterly Journal of the Royal Meteorological Society, 108*(455), 1–24. https://doi.org/10.1002/qj.49710845502

USGCRP, (2018). *Impacts, Risks, and Adaptation in the United States: Fourth National Climate Assessment*, Volume II: [Reidmiller, D.R., C.W. Avery, D.R. Easterling, K.E. Kunkel, K.L.M. Lewis, T.K. Maycock, and B.C. Stewart (eds.)]. U.S. Global Change Research Program, Washington, DC, USA, 1515 pp. doi: 10.7930/NCA4.2018. Published by U.S. Government Publishing Office Internet: bookstore.gpo.gov; Phone: toll free (866) 512-1800; DC area (202) 512-1800 Fax: (202) 512-2104 Mail: Stop IDCC, Washington, DC 20402-0001

Schalet, A. T., Tropp, L. R., & Troy, L. M. (2020). Making research usable beyond academic circles: A relational model of public engagement. *Analyses of Social Issues and Public Policy, 20*(1), 336–356. https://doi.org/10.1111/asap.12204

Shandas, V., Voelkel, J., Williams, J., & Hoffman, J. (2019). Integrating satellite and ground measurements for predicting locations of extreme urban heat. *Climate, 7*(1), 5. https://doi.org/10.3390/cli7010005

Shepherd, J. M., Pierce, H., & Negri, A. J. (2002). Rainfall modification by major urban areas: Observations from spaceborne rain radar on the TRMM satellite. *Journal of Applied Meteorology*, *41*(7), 689–701. https://doi.org/10.1175/1520-0450(2002)041<0689:RMBMUA>2.0.CO;2

Steinfeldt, T., Coil, C., & Plag, H.-P. (2015). *Understanding Virginia's vulnerability to climate change*. Mitigation & Adaptation Research Institute at Old Dominion University. Retrieved from https://digitalcommons.odu.edu/mari_documents/2

Stone, B. (2008). Urban sprawl and air quality in large US cities. *Journal of Environmental Management*, *86*(4), 688–698. https://doi.org/10.1016/j.jenvman.2006.12.034

Voelkel, J., Shandas, V., & Haggerty, B. (2016). Developing high-resolution descriptions of urban heat islands: A public health imperative. *Preventing Chronic Disease*, *13*, E129–E129. PubMed. https://doi.org/10.5888/pcd13.160099

Wilkening, S. (2021). *Museums and trust* (p. 56) [Audience Research]. American Alliance of Museums. Retrieved from www.aam-us.org/wp-content/uploads/2021/09/Museums-and-Trust-2021.pdf

Wilson, B. (2020). Urban heat management and the legacy of redlining. *Journal of the American Planning Association*, *86*(4), 443–457. https://doi.org/10.1080/01944363.2020.1759127

7 Conclusion
Common themes, lessons learned, and next steps

Vivek Shandas & Dana Hellman

Overview

A major theme in all the chapters of this book is the need for diverse stakeholders – in the present case, researchers and practitioners – to learn together. Learning together may seem obvious as many of us since grade school have been engaging in such activities, though obstacles in our individual institutions require careful articulation of the contours to achieve successful collaborations. Accordingly, the chapters herein represent an opportunity to learn from the challenges, successes, and continuing opportunities in advancing an equity-centered agenda for addressing climate change. As we reflect on these chapters, we ask a series of questions, including: Were these collaborations effective in addressing current inequities in climate change? Did they produce outcomes that were practically impactful, while advancing insights about future research and practice? Do these projects and partnerships have staying power?

Central to attaining the goals embedded within these questions is the ability to navigate institutional barriers, overcome existing systems of rewards and penalties, and make explicit the historic and often unstated precedents about 'staying in our lane.' The authors of this compendium exhibited, through their rich picture descriptions of individual case studies, an ability to span seemingly formidable boundaries in part because they see existing systems as unable to address the challenges of our time. In some instances, the authors were rebuked by institutional watchdogs, and faced the loss of professional position and reputation, or ability to continue with existing responsibilities. In all cases, managing logistical issues and the building of trust required formidable commitments of time and patience. The authors' heroic feats require recognition in their own right, while the ability to articulate the collaborative experience within the context of a book chapter is akin to the late Congressman John Lewis's notion of 'good trouble.' We start this conclusion with recognition of the contributions made by these authors and

DOI: 10.4324/9781003208723-7

the lessons they have helped us to highlight in addressing complex problems like climate change and social equity.

Boundary spanning

In summarizing this work, we identify a number of implications for understanding boundary spanning that follow from the preceding chapters. A central theme in conceptualizing collaborative processes among communities of practice is our ability to manage change through a recursive hierarchy of feedback processes that organize 'differences' into classes of social facts. Social practices such as climate collaborations entail the interaction and comparison of actions and traits that thereby either reinforce or challenge this system of distinction. In this case, the field of climate research is internally differentiated across disciplines within institutions of research (e.g., biology, urban planning, public policy), which means that there must already be some competence for boundary spanning among its constituent members, objects, and practices. Viewed more dynamically, the central practices of engaging in climate research or policy are 'remnants' of what were once marginal practices on the periphery of other fields, just as today's marginal practices could constitute part of tomorrow's central practices of an as-yet-unimagined community of practice. Whether we are engaged more with the research or practice (or both) components of the equation, we must strike a balance between differentiation from and communication with 'others.' To use the somewhat crude language of economics, partnerships form when the calculus shifts such that the benefits of increased communication and coordination outweigh the costs associated with reduced autonomy.

We observed this phenomenon in several cases throughout the previous chapters. For example, when the UREx SRN project, which comprised the basis for several of the present project descriptions, recognized that extensive interdisciplinary approaches within a university would only be useful to practices of climate change up to a certain point. UREx SRN projects aimed to create a 'sweet spot' where core competency and new experiences may serve one another, mutually reinforcing the need to expand the boundaries that have, in the past, constrained the ability for each community of practice to inform the other. Boundary spanning, as such, entails routine operations that reinforce the field – in the case of the UREx SRN projects, reinforcements occurred through topically focused research groups (e.g., hydrology, urban heat, modeling), which allowed for boundary spanning at the edges of specific domains of disciplinary knowledge and creating the conditions to potentially transform the entire field. The extent to which boundary spanning occurred then is a function of the specific community that engaged in the collaborative processes; that is, what may appear on one level to be truly transformative boundary spanning will appear at the next 'higher' (or 'deeper') level to be a routine social practice.

At the same time, a field of practice, such as emergency management or public policy, is always subject to change, in part because the communicative aspect of social practice also affords agents the opportunity, albeit constrained, to reflect on and negotiate the meaning of these relationships. The existing and routine social practices within a field of practice may not involve interaction or collaboration with researchers, yet doing so can bring together diverse practices and associated objects and agents in novel ways, which can generate 'artifacts of practice' that may have never been previously imagined. If those novel recombinations find sufficient technical and cultural support, they are likely to change the relations between those practices to form a new field of engagement, which we argue is the field of equity-based climate collaborations. The emergence of a new joint field of research and practice also changes the fields that participate in it. As more agents adopt the innovations of the joint field, these innovations become what Levina and Vaast (2005) refer to as 'boundary objects-in-use.' Some of the agents may themselves participate in the production of boundary objects-in-use to become 'boundary spanners-in-practice' (Levina & Vaast, 2005). More fundamentally, the relations between the fields will change, resulting in changes in the core practices and functions of those fields.

Enduring partnerships

Another theme that emerges is our ability to create enduring equity-based climate collaborations among researchers and practitioners. The case studies in the present book suggest to a reasonable level that the strength of the coupling between researchers and practitioners – the partnership capacity of the participating institutions – fall along a continuum. The literature supports this view by suggesting that effective partnerships manage the considerable uncertainties associated with networked governance by striking an appropriate balance between formal and informal rules as well as between weak and strong ties (e.g., Klijn & Koppenjan, 2015). Thus, we should expect effective researcher–practitioner partnerships will fall somewhere on the continuum between a loose collection of independent organizations where partnerships exist in name only, and dominant or strong partnerships where member organizations are essentially co-opted entities subject to the rules and reproductive requirements of a partnership bureaucracy. As such, partnerships that endure can be thought of as complex adaptive systems in which partnerships and their community co-evolve.

The form of complex adaptive and co-evolving partnerships are represented in the case studies as hybrid conditions characterized by a fluid exchange of agents, objects, and practices both among the local fields and between these fields and the partnership as a whole. In the Barrio Innovation approach described by Berbés-Blázquez et al., partnership began small and then scaled up across the entire school district. In this case, the boundaries between university researchers and school district practitioners seem to shift back and forth in their salience between local boundaries (i.e., smaller-scale pilot projects), and the partnership boundary (i.e., across the whole school district). This stands in contrast to Hoffman et al., who described a network of partnerships that crossed through government, academic, and nonprofit sectors to include organizations whose mission was even tangentially related to acting on extreme urban heat. In this case, the boundary spanning processes recognized the importance of generating a locally relevant dataset that could be used to prioritize limited resources to maximum effect. In both cases, while taking seemingly different approaches, the durability of the partnerships neither completely governs the institutional ecologies nor are they completely governed by it; rather, they are interdependent.

Sustaining enduring partnerships also requires the ability to manage change, which was mentioned by several authors. Changes across collaborations are inevitable, and vital partnerships set community agendas and as much as follow them. If partnership changes are allowed to somehow inform project goals or, similarly, management of perceived discrepancies, then a resulting dynamic partnership seems to have the capacity to precipitate and thereby control changes in its relevant socio-technical and policy environment. But just as importantly, the mutual adjustment of boundary spanning and core practices helps to ensure that partnership goals remain grounded in local contexts of practice. In the case of Hermosillo, Robles-Morúa et al. describe changes in the participation of municipal authorities, and yet, the core principles of participating researchers providing climate information not readily available to planners and municipal directors seemed to maintain the collaboration. Similarly, the Barrio Innovation approach established a common set of principles and progressive social baseline that allowed participants to work well together, including a 'will to experiment and the will to change course.' In other words, being adaptive was essential. Perhaps particularly in the contemporary policy context, such researcher–practitioner collaborations that endure are the ones that can strike this balance between being adaptive and consistent; visionary but still relevant to present partners and issues.

Future directions

Despite the extraordinary contributions made by the authors of these chapters, the field of researcher–practitioner collaboration within climate change is still in its infancy. As we have seen attempts at creating global compacts on climate collaborations, such as UN Climate Change Conferences (COPs), these are not easy and require tenacity and commitment. With challenges at a global scale, these case studies suggest a need for a cannon of literature emphasizing partnerships that span institutional boundaries and aim to improve our adaptation potential from the hyperlocal scale upward/outward. These early cases, while exhibiting promise in terms of advancing local climate actions and engaging researchers and practitioners, recognize that we are still early in the understanding of climate collaborations. Issues of equity, which are a result of institutional processes that arguably did conduct the level of boundary spanning necessary, are a result of the recalcitrant norms and silos that currently make up climate research and practice. Indeed, through this process we have learned that several questions remain unanswerable based on the evidence available in this compendium.

We note that the case studies are of individual places, and that they are often idiosyncratic to the needs of society. As such, we still do not know the extent to which these climate collaborations are scalable to other parts of the world that are not part of this book. Several cross-sectoral projects, for example, the ERASMUS+ out of the European Commission and South Asia Heat Health Information Network, show promise in their collaborations, and also share many of the thematic boundary spanning similarities showcased here. Our ability to advance some of the findings around climate collaborations may arguably be limited to those who already recognize the challenges facing collective actions on grand challenges, like climate change. Still unknown are the extent to which the tools, resources, and processes offered in this book provide a compelling, accessible, and useful approach to communities who do not share the same persuasions about a warming planet. For example, how might tools such as scenario planning support the collective learning about how to engage communities unfamiliar with boundary spanning collaborations? What of those practitioners who have reservations about working with climate researchers – do they need to be part of a network like the UREx SRN to fully participate and benefit from such collective endeavors? Similarly, are these tools and approaches relevant to community members who self-identify as residents and not experts in terms of climate or policies? The ability for us to expand and create a more inclusive approach to conducting climate collaborations will likely depend on the processes and contexts for engaging participations, which is another area of future research.

Finally, we recognize that as new information emerges and the climate changes, so will the sectors that work together. At this point, climate researchers and practitioners are supporting the earliest of local policies and programs to safeguard communities. We currently have a limited idea for how this field of climate collaboration will evolve and in what ways other sectors, for example, the private sector partners and military operations will participate in these discussions. As the field changes so will the participants, which means that understanding the processes for engaging in climate collaborations will also need to evolve. Tools that are currently used in other fields of research and practice can be brought together to engage emerging sectors of participants.

The urgency of finding effective collaborations within the climate field is worth noting. Immediate suggestions for communities to advance climate collaborations include developing explicit understanding of the roles and responsibilities of participants; creating realistic timelines that honor different institutional cultures yet also move toward developing effective practices; enabling junior and senior participants to engage in ways that are differently supported; and developing a theory of change that is grounded in a contextual understanding of the assets and opportunities in a region. The perceived value of undertaking collaborations of this nature is twofold. First, as we have argued, the efforts of researchers and practitioners can be highly complementary, with the latter facilitating community connections and tangible outputs, and the former grounding climate concerns in science, data, and transferable theory. These results have significant implications for the promise of climate *action*, as opposed to inquiry, concern, or good intentions. Naturally then, a secondary measure of collaborative value is the extent to which partnerships might inform and enable elusive funding mechanisms that make desired climate- and equity-related interventions a reality. Financial resources are scarce, and it is important to direct funds toward the most vulnerable communities or urgent issues. Programs and adaptation strategies deployed with the precision of research behind them may prove more impactful, apposite, and cost-effective, improving conditions on the ground while furthering scholarship. Collaborative relationships are essential, mutually beneficial, and hold great promise for the future of climate adaptation and equity, particularly when their dynamics become clearer and their benefits more seamlessly leveraged.

References

Klijn, E. H., & Koppenjan, J. (2015). *Governance networks in the public sector*. Abingdon, UK: Routledge. https://doi.org/10.4324/9781315887098

Levina, N., & Vaast, E. (2005). The emergence of boundary spanning competence in practice: Implications for implementation and use of information systems. *MIS Quarterly*, *29*(2), 335–363.

For Product Safety Concerns and Information please contact our EU representative GPSR@taylorandfrancis.com
Taylor & Francis Verlag GmbH, Kaufingerstraße 24, 80331 München, Germany

www.ingramcontent.com/pod-product-compliance
Lightning Source LLC
Chambersburg PA
CBHW051756230426
43670CB00012B/2315